M 12a

By the Same Author

A House Unlocked

PENELOPE LIVELY

VIKING

VIKING

Published by the Penguin Group
Penguin Books Ltd, 80 Strand, London WC2 0RL, England
Penguin Putnam Inc., 375 Hudson Street, New York, New York 10014, USA
Penguin Books Australia Ltd, Ringwood, Victoria, Australia
Penguin Books Canada Ltd, 10 Alcorn Avenue, Toronto, Ontario, Canada M4V 3B2
Penguin Books India (P) Ltd, 11 Community Centre,
Panchsheel Park, New Delhi – 110 017, India
Penguin Books (NZ) Ltd, Cnr Rosedale and Airborne Roads, Albany, Auckland, New Zealand
Penguin Books (South Africa) (Pty) Ltd, 5 Watkins Street,
Denver Ext 4, Johannesburg 2094, South Africa

Penguin Books Ltd, Registered Offices: 80 Strand, London WC2 0RL, England

First published 2001
1

Set in 12/14.75pt Monotype Dante
Typeset by Rowland Phototypesetting Ltd, Bury St Edmunds, Suffolk
Printed in Great Britain by Clays Ltd, St Ives plc

A CIP catalogue record for this book is available from the British Library

ISBN 0–670–89954–2

122,521
£19.50

IN MEMORY
J. F. L., B. M. R., R. B. R.

Contents

Preface

It has always seemed to me that one effective way of writing fiction is to take the immediate and particular and to give it a universal resonance – to so manipulate and expand personal experience that it becomes relevant to others. This book is an attempt to do the same thing not with a human life but with the span of one family's occupation of a house.

The house as I knew it exists now only in the mind. In my head, I can still move easily and vividly around it. The furnishings are precise and clear, the sounds and smells are as they ever were. I can walk through the front door into the vestibule, and thence into the hall. Ahead of me, the garden door frames a green section of Somerset; wisteria pours down above the veranda. I turn left past the gong stand and through into the dining-room, where I pause to look at the sunset picture above the sideboard, whose right-hand cupboard is minus its key and has to be opened by means of a piece of string . . . If I walk along the passage to the drawing-room the Turkish rug will skid under my feet on the parquet floor; when I open the door the sunlight will throw a mesh of shadow on to the framed sampler in its stand by the fireplace, with the row of embroidered children from Stepney.

This mansion in the mind, with its many rooms, each complete with furnishings – pictures and vases and pin-trays and the contents of drawers – seems to me an eerie personal reflection of those imaginary constructions of another age, the mnemonic devices of the classical and medieval art of memory.

Frances Yates's fine book on that subject describes the system whereby the sequence of an oratorical argument was retained by means of the creation of an imaginary mansion, within which the orator moved from room to room, each space serving as a stage in the argument, and the emotive trappings – a statue, an urn, a painting – acting as prompts for specific flights of language.

In the same way, I can move around my memory house and focus upon different objects. The house itself becomes a prompt – a system of reference, an assemblage of coded signs. Its contents conjure up a story; they are not the stations of an oratorical argument, but signifiers for the century.

Golsoncott, an Edwardian country house in the corner of west Somerset that lies between the Brendon hills and Exmoor, was the family home of my grandmother, Beatrice Reckitt (*née* Hewett), from 1923, when she and my grandfather bought it, until her death in 1975. Her daughter, the artist Rachel Reckitt, lived there until she died in 1995. I have known it all my life and spent most of my adolescence there.

The family's occupation of the house nearly covers the century – seventy years of social change. In 1923 its daily running required the services of eleven people; by the 1990s this infrastructure was remembered only in the wages book buried in the hall chest, in the bell system in the pantry, in the gong stand and the tarnished contents of the silver cupboard.

The house was fingered by the cataclysmic events of our time – the Russian Revolution, the Holocaust, the Blitz. My grandmother gave help and hospitality to a Russian family who had fled the aftermath of 1917; Mary Britnieva, the mother, wrote her hectic account of those years while staying at Golsoncott. Otto Kun, a fifteen-year-old Viennese refugee from the Nazis in 1939, was brought to Somerset by my aunt

Rachel and stayed for a while at Golsoncott. In 1940 the house became an official war nursery, with a group of children from London's East End billeted in the old staff wing.

When the potent process of dismemberment and dispersal became unavoidable after my aunt's death, the entire place – its furnishings, its functions – seemed like a set of coded allusions to a complex sequence of social change and historical clamour. Objects had proved more tenacious than people – the photograph albums, the baffling contents of the silver cupboard, the children on my grandmother's sampler of the house – but from each object there spun a shining thread of reference, if you knew how to follow it. I thought that I would see if the private life of a house could be made to bear witness to the public traumas of a century.

The Hall Chest, the Photograph Albums
and the Picnic Rug

The hall chest was carved oak, some four feet long and three feet deep. Late nineteenth-century, I would guess, and brought to Golsoncott from my grandparents' previous home in St Albans. Indeed, it features in a photograph in one of the albums, doing duty in that other hall. At Golsoncott the chest housed the albums, a great pile of them, the hefty leather-bound objects favoured in the early part of the twentieth century. Here was the pictorial history of the house and garden, and their predecessors at St Albans; through the pages troop family and friends, from the 1890s onwards. Edwardian skirts and Norfolk jackets give way to twenties shapeless dresses and Oxford bags. People are decked out in silks and morning dress for weddings; young mothers pose with babies by the sundial in the rose garden. The babies grow up and are wed in turn; more babies peer down into the lily pond.

At the other end of the chest was a welter of dog leads, brown wrapping paper, lengths of string and bald tennis balls. On the top of the contents lay the picnic rug, stained and weathered tartan, veteran of many a moorland lunch or tea and potent symbol of how it all began – the family's hundred-year addiction to north-west Somerset, now into the fifth generation.

You could say that this addiction was fuelled by the advent of the Great Western Railway. Wordsworth and Coleridge had a hand in it, which would perhaps have been news to my grandmother and her siblings – not a bookish lot – whooping it up on the moor in their youth around the turn of the century. There they are, the Hewetts, in the earliest album, the late Victorian family incarnate, their names alone pinning them firmly to a time and a class: Walter, Gilbert, Maud, Beatrice, Harold and Douglas. On a Sunday afternoon in 1895, having tea on the lawn of Wootton Courtenay Rectory, rented for the summer, the party expanded with a couple of friends. Most of them are sitting on chairs, but the two youngest are sprawled on a rug similar to the one I knew in my adolescence. There is a table with white cloth and silver kettle; on the grass is a three-tier cake stand, the cakes largely demolished. The girls – all are in their late teens or early twenties – wear hats, round straw with shallow crowns and brims and wide petersham bands. All have long skirts and sumptuously swollen leg-of-mutton sleeves, either on their white-frilled and pin-tucked blouses worn with a dark ribbon tied in a bow around the neck, or on their jackets. Other photographs are less posed – here they are on Larkbarrow in the autumn of 1901, on a moorland hike, in deerstalkers and straw boaters, Norfolk jackets and long skirts. Here is Harold in a larky pose with his head on one side and boater tipped jauntily to the back of his head, beside his nicely smiling sisters, a pipe jutting incongruously from his youthful face. And here he is flat on his back on the shingle of Porlock beach with Maud leaning over him, bespectacled and wearing a man's tie, apparently admonishing. Often some or all of them are on horseback – the horse always named in the handwritten caption: Lorna, Hard Bargain. Dogs too are meticulously identified.

In all these photographs the family is defined by dress. What they wear and how and where they are wearing it tells you who they are: upper class. They may be on holiday, in an isolated spot, engaged in strenuous country pursuits, but they cannot be without their badges of identity. The girls must have their matching coats and skirts, their hats, the men their tweed jackets, their collars and ties. Looking at family parties in summer Somerset today, I note that everyone is again clad very much alike – in jeans, leggings, chinos, T-shirts, trainers. But nothing tells me where the wearers fit into the social system – they are classless, anonymous. Until they open their mouths, and even then distinctions are blurred. Back in 1900 that family's dress and utterance set them apart instantly. Anyone seeing and hearing them could have told you what sort of home they occupied and their manner of living.

The story of Golsoncott over the seventy years of its occupancy by this family has two dominating themes, and those are social change and absence of change. The style of its habitation over time reflects in microcosm the shifting sands of this country's class structure. Things are done differently now – up to a point. The structure remains, but at the end of the twentieth century it is opaque, furtive, lurking behind the engineering feats of educational opportunity and social mobility. We all know who we are and whence we came, but it is harder to define others. This subtle reconstruction of how people view one another is nicely expressed, for me, in those sepia photographs of six twenty-somethings on Exmoor back then.

Sepia. A descriptive term for a kind of early photograph, but also a loaded one. The photographs themselves are loaded, indeed. I have to look at them with a cool dissecting eye because images such as these are tainted. They have become the currency of the remembrance industry – the stock of grainy postcards for sale by the bundle, the furnishings of souvenir guidebooks, representing a past that is reinvented in tune with the requirements of the present. Heritage. Nostalgia. Freighted words – nostalgia especially, a term itself subject to reinterpretation over time. Pejorative today, implying a distorted vision to be avoided, but a term that carried a clear and precise meaning once, in the eighteenth century: 'homesickness', German *Heimweh*, a condition recognized as requiring treatment and thus, when diagnosed in a soldier, entitling him to a spell of home leave.

So I look at the photographs for what they can tell me about their time, trying to extract information, to see beyond the obscuring sepia haze that gives them nostalgia status. But they have a further dimension. Those people fossilized in that particular fraction of a second subsequently stepped out of the frame, assumed flesh and personality. Several of them are vibrant within my own head – my grandmother, my great-uncles – reconstructed for the 1950s, '60s and '70s. Nostalgia in any sense of the term is out of place.

Four members of that turn-of-the-century group would eventually settle in west Somerset. My grandmother brought her family there in 1923 to Golsoncott, a Lutyens-style house built some ten or fifteen years earlier at the foot of the Brendon Hills, and set about creating a large Gertrude Jekyll-style garden to complement it. Aunt Maud set herself up in a gloomy house in Porlock that matched her aloof, acerbic style – I remember visits to her in adolescence, neither of us finding anything to say to the other. Douglas and Harold, the youngest of the siblings, became Uncle Chuff and Uncle Herk, pursuing brief parallel careers in the Burmese and Indian Civil Services before retiring at a comfortably early age to live together in a house overlooking Porlock Vale, purpose-built for them before such refinements as planning permission. They were bachelors in the old-fashioned sense of the word – not a woman in sight, nor anything else. Their long and gleeful retirement was devoted entirely to walking and riding on the moor, rising to the seasonal high of stag hunting, on which Uncle Herk published a small but definitive work, *The Fairest Hunting*. The house was astonishing, a cross between a London club and an officers' mess somewhere in the East – huge battered leather armchairs, brass coffee tables, moth-eaten oriental rugs, bamboo screens, a tiger skin. Bits of foxes and stags sprouted from the wall – grinning masks, tattered brushes, a forest of antlers. We used to go there for tea – the uncles served copious schoolboy teas: jam puffs, doughnuts, sponge rolls, rock cakes. They wore ancient hairy tweeds deeply impregnated with cigarette smoke. Uncle Chuff was purple-faced and convivial, Uncle Herk was beaky, weather-beaten and equipped with a silver cigarette case on the back of which each fag was briskly tapped before being lit. They addressed each other as 'brother' and my grandmother as 'sister', treating her with joshing affection, as someone deeply familiar but of another species. And, looking again at the photographs, I see that she and Maud are always standing together but slightly apart from the others. Their brothers in plus-fours and jackets are a uniformed brigade: the Men.

My great-uncles seem to have hammered their sex drive into total submission and settled to a satisfactorily uncomplicated alternative of pursuing red deer over the moor. I remember them fondly and admire their genial treatment of a young and awkward female relative – they can't have had much to do with schoolgirls. Indeed, when I knew them in the forties and fifties they had not had much to do with a good deal of twentieth-century England, holed up down there, and hence were relatively untroubled by what was going on elsewhere. There were ritual fulminations about the horrors of a Labour government after 1945, but with a certain detachment, as though they could not conceive that they themselves would be severely inconvenienced, as indeed they probably were not. Rather surprisingly, both of them went in for versifying – carefully typed selections survive still, some of them dating back to 1900. Cod verses after Tennyson and Kipling. Heavy-handed Edwardian humour – 'Apology to a Lady' makes you wonder for a moment about their bachelordom: 'If you met an angel / You would surely find / You for once had lost your head / Got confused in mind / Now perhaps you understand / Why I always put / Into every social trap / My ungainly foot.' But another poem by Uncle Herk sets the record straight by pondering the advantages of marriage, and then deciding that his horse is preferable as a companion – biddable, controllable and, it would seem, more congenial. A somewhat ham-handed Longfellow parody has Hiawatha out with the Devon and Somerset staghounds and failing to be in at the kill: 'Very wroth was Hiawatha / To have missed the glorious finish.' But a high proportion of their verse is jingoistic stuff hymning the glories of Empire and the virtues of being English. I read it now with bewilderment, thinking of those jovial figures, plying one with jam tarts and talking to my grandmother about their dahlias – realizing that the climate of their minds is as alien as that of another century.

The attractions of Exmoor and west Somerset for those turn-of-the-century young people were sternly physical. They would pursue their favourite activities – riding, walking, cycling. Walking, above all – punishing long-distance walks across the moor, the ritual morning ramble. My grandmother considered a daily walk an essential part of civilized existence – she continued the regime into her eighties and lived to the age of ninety-seven. In the Golsoncott cloakroom was a stack of walking-sticks, their handles burnished with use, the necessary props for swiping nettles, lifting gate latches, hooking down a high spray of blackberries. The family took walking seriously, and in that sense they were eerie descendants of those great walkers, the Romantic poets, and also precursors of the early twentieth-century passion for hiking and rambling, when striding out into the landscape ceased to be a middle-class preserve and became a leisure occupation for the masses. Type the keyword 'rambles' into the British Library on-line catalogue for publications before 1975 and up come a dizzying 969 entries, some indication of the spread and intensity of interest. In the twenties and thirties the urban young and fit poured out into the countryside, on cycles and on foot, perfectly enshrined by those Shell posters of the period in which rosy-cheeked figures in shorts, shirts and hiking boots pause to consult the map on a five-barred gate.

But that particular revolution was a long way off in the 1890s. Walking for pleasure was a socially restricted activity. Furthermore, Exmoor itself was a relatively recent discovery, opened up by the railway in much the same way as the Rocky Mountains or the Sierra Nevada. People had not realized it was there – except of course those who had been living and working in those parts for centuries. But from the moment Isambard Kingdom Brunel's line snaked west towards the toe of the country, and in due course threw out tentacles to net the whole of the peninsula, nothing would be the same again.

My great-grandparents were West Country holiday pioneers, beneficiaries of the Great Western Railway. At the turn of the century they started to remove there with their brood, renting a house and settling in for a season of determined activity. Exmoor was ideal – it had overtones of Scotland but was now more accessible and was furnished with equivalent fauna, some of which you could slaughter on horseback rather than with a gun, thus combining two favoured activities, riding and blood sports. The men shot, rode and walked. The women walked and sketched. They were after all late Victorians and knew what was expected of them – my grandmother indeed went briefly to art college in London (where she attended classes given by Gilbert Tonks) and had a talent which was later expressed in superb needlework. But, most importantly, they were celebrating the scenic glories of the place – the great curves of the moor, the melting colours, the green tapestry of the combes. West Somerset had arrived as somewhere you visited for aesthetic enjoyment.

It had not always been so. For centuries discriminating travellers seldom set foot further west than Bristol and Bath and those who did steered well clear of the barren wastes of Exmoor and Dartmoor. The ecstatic discovery of the Quantocks by Coleridge and the Wordsworths was the beginning of the gathering perception through the nineteenth century that there was much to be said for points west, but initially this was a revelation restricted to a small number of *cognoscenti*. Philip Gosse trawled for seashore specimens on the north Devon coast. The Tennysons visited Lynton on their honeymoon and explored the Valley of the Rocks. Large-scale visitation of the area was still a long way off; the three counties, Somerset, Devon and Cornwall, got on with what they had been doing for centuries, agriculture and local industry – a world apart. The moorland was simply there, the soft grey ridge on the horizon – rising from green distances and crowned with a fleece of cloud along its length – that one sees from the train today.

Early topographical travel writers steered clear of the moor. Celia Fiennes, indomitably riding west in 1698, ignores it entirely as she travels from Taunton to Wellington and Cullompton and thence deeper into Devon. The charms of Exeter merit several pages ('spacious noble streets and a vast trade is carried on') and the plunging Devon hills are noted in passing but the distantly looming moor is of no apparent interest. Daniel Defoe was also inclined to focus on town descriptions but with a distinctly wider range and depth; and he did at least notice the moor, travelling north-west from Taunton to take a look at the coast and thus, by the way, 'Exmore [which] gives, indeed, but a melancholy view, being a vast tract of barren, and desolate lands; yet on the coast, there are some very good sea-ports.' He also nails the perceived otherness of the west with his comments on local speech in Somerset:

It cannot pass my observation here, that when we are come this length from London, the dialect of the English tongue, or the country way of expressing themselves is not easily understood, it is so strangely altered; it is true that it is so in many parts of England besides, but in none so gross a degree as in this part.

Later eighteenth-century travellers paid hardly any attention to areas off the beaten track. Dr Richard Pococke was a clergyman whose duties were sufficiently undemanding to allow for frequent and extended travels. Indeed, he cut his teeth as a travel writer with the grandly titled *A Description of the East and Some Other Countries*, an account of a journey to Egypt and the Levant. But in later life he concentrated on home territory with *Travels through England*, a busy and informative survey which included a tour right down through the West Country into Cornwall. He sticks to the south coast of Devon, sternly (or wisely) avoiding the interior and is mainly interested in cathedrals, castles, the seats of the aristocracy and country gentry. He was writing with an eye to his readership, presumably, and was well aware that they would be no more inclined than he himself was to risk a foray into the wastes of the moor.

But there is also the crucial matter of aesthetic taste and fashion. Neither Exmoor nor the Quantocks had achieved the essential qualifying factor of the time for serious inspection. They were not classified as 'picturesque'. The Revd William Gilpin, whose writings were so influential in focusing the interest of discerning late eighteenth-century tourists, concentrated on the Lake District and the Wye Valley. Those were the chosen perfect places, where the visitor might examine landscape 'by the rules of picturesque beauty: that of not merely describing; but of adapting the description of natural scenery to the principles of artificial landscape; and of opening the sources of those pleasures, which are derived from the comparison.' The philosophy of the picturesque emphasized the search for scenes of natural beauty that rose to the requirements of artistic composition and indeed in Gilpin's more robust interpretations warranted definite interference. The obstinately rigid lines of some parts of Tintern Abbey annoyed him: 'A mallet judiciously used . . . might be of service in fracturing some of them . . .' Ruins could be more easily manipulated than those other stalwarts of the picturesque scene – mountains, lakes, cascades, the play of light and shade, the glow of sunset. The sensitive traveller thus sought out views in which such factors met their most ideal combination. A flood of publications gave guidance in the last half of the century and conditioned the vision and the opinions of commentators, amongst them Arthur Young. He himself ventured no further west than Bristol and Bath in his tour of southern England, though he dutifully visited Monmouth and Chepstow to marvel at the Severn and the Wye valleys and registered all the correct responses: 'what makes the whole picture perfect, is its being entirely surrounded by vast rocks and precipices, covered thick with wood . . . nothing has so glorious an effect, as breaking unexpectedly upon a cascade, gushing from the rocks, and overhung with wood'. He goes a step further with stern criticisms of the artificially created picturesque walk at Persfield, on the Wye, which in his view falls short of the received requirements at some points – this from a man whose main concern and reason for travel is agricultural practice, crop rotation and breeds of cattle. If you saw with a late eighteenth-century eye and wanted to rate as a person with taste, you could see in one way only.

For most earlier travellers, the perfect landscape was man-made. Celia Fiennes disliked the Pennines and the Lake District. Dr Johnson deplored the 'hopeless sterility' of the Scottish Highlands. Ordered fertility was the ideal – cornfields, fat cattle and the symmetry imposed by the Enclosure Acts. This attitude remained widespread throughout the eighteenth century and beyond, but alongside it grew a more specialist taste for nature and wilderness, encouraged by the cult of the picturesque and fed by a familiarity with European art – including the paintings of Claude, Salvator Rosa, Poussin. The Lake District and the Wye Valley became Meccas for the sophisticated traveller, along with the Scottish Highlands and the mountains of Wales. And in due course the conviction of many eighteenth-century commentators that manipulation of nature was essential in order to achieve picturesque perfection gave way to the romantic idealization of the untouched natural scene. But the remorseless spread of agriculture meant that uncontaminated nature was increasingly hard to find. Wild and romantic scenery had been all but obliterated by the neat fields and browsing cattle that were once the ideal landscape. Those ultimate connoisseurs, the Romantic poets, looked west and saw the Quantocks and Exmoor rising from the agricultural order and fertility of Somerset like symbols of the apposition between nature and human intervention.

Exmoor was not picturesque – its rolling skyline being short on peaks and gradients, devoid of lakes, its cascades not up to Lake District standards. The eighteenth century ignored the place, to all intents and purposes. It took the pioneer enthusiasm of Coleridge to put it on the map – or at least on the highly select map of the nineteenth century *littérateur* – bouncing into Nether Stowey in 1797 and then dragging the Wordsworths there to share with him the delights of the Quantocks. But literary vision is capable of wide and potent dissemination over time and space. Poetry above all becomes so interwoven with place that a landscape can take on an enhanced identity for ever after. My grandmother had no great literary inclinations but she knew what was appropriate. ' "Where Alph, the sacred river, ran . . ." ' she would declaim, stumping along the cliff path through the woods from Porlock to Culbone, ' "Through caverns measureless to man . . ." Over to you!' That was as far as she could get, and anyway I was supposed to be the bookish one. The Romantic poets did not directly take my grandmother's contemporaries to west Somerset but they created the climate of mind that would eventually send them in that direction. Coleridge's opium-ridden night at Ash Farm above Culbone was to resonate in curious ways. A poem was fuelled by his vision of those woods and cliffs, but the place subsequently claimed the poet. For generations of visitors the area would be mysteriously incandescent with some hidden code of reference – half-remembered, half-known. In the summer of 1997 a white hoarding marched bold black letters along the side of a warehouse on Watchet's docks: 'The fair breeze blew, the white foam flew, the furrow followed free.'

Poets expand our vision. Specific landscapes seem to require the endorsement of literary recognition. West Somerset had the good fortune to lure that unique group in the dying years of the eighteenth century; a hundred years later the poets' fleeting passage and its enduring legacy had lent depth and resonance to those hills and woods, that coast. Another century on, and it is the same.

According to Dorothy Wordsworth, the idea for 'The Rime of the Ancient Mariner' was born on a winter walk from Quantoxhead by way of Watchet to Dulverton. Some seventeen miles, that must have been. Nothing exceptional by Romantic poet hiking standards. Coleridge walked from Nether Stowey south through the Vale of Taunton and over the Blackdown Hills to visit the Wordsworths at Racedown in Dorset. The coastal walk from the Quantocks to Lynton was a particular favourite – a ninety-mile round-trip made by Coleridge with the Wordsworths, with Hazlitt and on his own (on one occasion completing the trip in two consecutive days). He walked to Bristol, to Cheddar. Cross-country journeys that ignored the inconvenience of inadequate turnpikes, about which travellers such as Arthur Young and William Cobbett grumble so bitterly, and that kept the walker in intimate contact with the landscape – with its gradients, its vegetation, its waterways, and of course with all the refinements of natural splendour which were essential inspirational material. The topographical writers of the seventeenth and eighteenth centuries were on horseback (hence the turnpike problem); the poets chose to walk – taking the immemorial way of moving around the country, engaging with it mile by mile as a medieval pedlar would have done, or a Saxon arrival, or a Bronze Age trader. And in so doing they gave to walking a new validity – the Romantic touch. It would cease to be a purely functional activity and take on overtones of something else, uplifting, reviving. You didn't have to be a poet for walking to enlarge the spirit – you prospered just as much from it as late Victorian gentry or twentieth-century urban workers.

The young Hewetts holidayed on Exmoor year after year, with occasional forays to Scotland. And, in the case of my grandmother and her sister, across the Channel. The Grand Tour was at its last gasp by 1900 but their trips to France and Italy, both then and later in my grandmother's life, exactly reflected the Tour's purpose and aspirations. You went abroad to look at art and architecture; such travel was essential education and improvement. I caught a last whiff of it myself in the late 1940s, towed round the Romanesque churches of central and southern France, my aunt determinedly seeking out every remote crumbling edifice, and my grandmother equipped with a supply of Ryvita, sandwich spread, Marmite and Ovaltine for the point when she could no longer endure unremitting French cuisine.

But the intervening forty years had brought a revolution to the concept of travel and above all to the concept of 'abroad'. One aspect of it has been aptly called the solar revolution. The Victorian and Edwardian traveller avoided the sun. A tan had unacceptable connotations, both social and racial; the sun was a menace and accordingly you kept out of it or protected yourself with hats and parasols. Equally, there was nothing wrong with grey English skies – a spot of rain did no one any harm. By 1940 this outlook had been turned on its head. The twenties and thirties saw the surge of sun culture, filtering down from the hedonistic writing of the day – by Norman Douglas, D. H. Lawrence, Robert Graves and others – and creating an obsession with heat, beaches, blue skies, the Mediterranean. By the time I was a schoolgirl the cult of abroad and the parallel dismissal of England was at its height. 'No lovely abroad for us this year . . .' sighs the woman strapped for cash in Angus Wilson's *Hemlock and After*. It is an attitude I remember keenly – the ferocious competition for discovery of uncontaminated Greek islands, Spanish fishing villages, charming French backwaters. If you were reduced one year to slinking off to Cornwall or the Suffolk coast, you kept quiet about it. Abroad was more scenic, richer in aesthetic experience, and the weather was much better. Abroad, the rural working class became a colourful peasantry and the urban crowds a stimulating spectacle. Abroad, you yourself blossomed and expanded. The travel writing of the day was a cult – no self-respecting coffee-table was complete without a copy of *Bitter Lemons* or the latest Patrick Leigh Fermor.

I had grown up in Egypt. Abroad was the norm for me and I didn't quite see what the fuss was about, looking at England with the eyes of a newcomer and the appreciative vision of youth. What I saw seemed both beautiful and interesting, as I moved through my adolescence. There were rural landscapes and medieval churches here too – why were those on the other side of the Channel so necessarily superior? But I was out of step with the times. It has been edifying to live on into an age when Sunday newspapers can run travel pieces on Norfolk or Wales and still hold up their heads in polite society – let alone to see a hefty suntan eyed with misgivings, albeit for a rather different reason.

There is also the question of what constitutes travel. The word itself has mutated. Today travel suggests distance, it implies leaving these shores – the notion of 'abroad' is implicit. In the late nineteenth century that was not necessarily so. The promotional literature of the Great Western Railway makes this clear. A gazetteer of 1906 – serving as a kind of pioneer

West Country AA / RAC / Good Hotel / Farm Holiday Guide rolled into one and clearly aimed at a wide market – subtly lures the reader by advocating the annual holiday as an essential palliative to the stress of modern living:

What was once a question of caprice and luxury is now a necessity if the danger of a breakdown is to be avoided . . . A century ago holiday-making as we now understand it was practically the monopoly of the rich. 'The Grand Tour of Europe' (performed either in lumbering diligences or little less cumbersome coaches) was, like a yearly visit to Bath, looked upon as part and parcel of fashionable life. The former, at any rate, was a condition precedent to the completion of a polite education. With very few exceptions . . . the whole of rural England (though possessing natural, historical and climatic attractions of the highest order) was one vast and neglected *terra incognita*. A pilgrimage to Rome could be accomplished with greater ease than a visit to St David's; it was less expensive to go to Paris than to journey to Penzance . . . The storm and stress of life have increased commensurately with the rapid evolution of travelling facilities, and it is indeed fortunate that at the beginning of the twentieth century the indispensable modicum of quiet, rest, change and recreation can be obtained *at all seasons of the year* without either going abroad or spending a fortune.

By grace of God and the Great Western Railway. The sub-text here is clear: travel is no longer the perquisite of the nobs, you too can have your fair share, and what's more you owe it to yourself. And another thing: whence the insistence on the superiority of foreign parts? Look at the undiscovered country near at hand!

That being said, these early guides to the West Country display a certain unease. They cannot quite allow it to stand up for itself but have to vaunt its charms in terms of somewhere readily appreciated. Dunster is variously the Nuremberg of Wessex and the Alnwick of the west. Wells is rather startlingly identified as the Bruges of western England. The Grand Tour spread a long shadow. Literary pedigree is seized upon. The Ship Inn at Porlock can claim Coleridge, Wordsworth and Southey as *habitués*, according to the GWR's *Wonderful Wessex* of 1908.

The Railway Illustrated Guide of 1891 also ropes in Southey to endorse the splendours of the Valley of the Rocks:

Imagine a narrow vale between two ridges of rock covered with huge stones, the bare northern ridge looking like the very bones and skeletons of the earth-rock, imprisoning rock-stone held in thrall by other stone – the whole forming a huge, terrific, stupendously grand mass. I never felt the sublimity of solitude until I stood alone in the Valley of the Rocks.

Even more helpful is R. D. Blackmore's novel *Lorna Doone*, with its lavish descriptions of Exmoor and a luridly romantic story. Exmoor became Doone country, given further validation by fiction.

Lank Combe running down to Badgworthy Water is still labelled 'Doone Country' on some of today's maps; road signs also announce entry to this mythical and literary region. The majority of contemporary tourists are no doubt mystified. Those to whom the name means anything will probably know it from guidebooks and brochures. As it has been ever since its 1869 publication, R. D. Blackmore's novel is still in print, today in editions polarized between that with a scholarly introduction and editorial notes and brash curtailed versions for children. I doubt if it is much read in either form. But *Lorna*

Doone was the great late Victorian blockbuster, outselling *The History of Henry Esmond Esq.* or *The Cloister and the Hearth*, running through forty editions in its first forty years of life, with the 1911 edition marking over 760,000 sales. Its popularity continued further into the first half of the twentieth century, though by the mid century many editions were abridgements – the reading public had lost the stomach for a Victorian three-decker.

Its success was phenomenal, startling its author who was always a touch peeved that his fourteen other novels sank far behind, let alone his poetry and his translation of Virgil's *Georgics*. *Lorna Doone* is a historical romance, but it is also a regional novel, precisely located in identifiable Exmoor land-scape, and it is as such that it brought visitors to the area by the thousand, intent upon finding the watersplash up which young John Ridd climbed to his first encounter with the child Lorna and the church in which she was shot by Carver Doone as she stood beside John at the altar. It has all the essential ingredients for popularity – strong narrative, adventure, arresting characters and a vibrant love interest – and must have been enjoyed by a wide spectrum of Victorian and Edwardian readers, including those for whom reading was not a central activity, such as my grandmother and her family. Significantly, the horse ridden by my great-grandfather in one photograph is named Lorna.

For the contemporary reader, the novel is imbued with Victorian values, despite its seventeenth-century setting. Lorna is the archetypal Victorian child-woman heroine, John Ridd the worthy and hard-working farmer who advances himself to an eventual knighthood after an adroit display of selfless courage – thereby making himself a more suitable match for the aristocratic Lorna. City and country are set in apposition, with rural Exmoor as the idealized Arcadia which the lovers eventually achieve once more after an enforced spell amid the corruptions of London. There is even a side-swipe at the evils of industrialization in the depiction of an ill-fated and exploitative mining venture in the wastes of the moor. The Doones themselves are something of a puzzle – not just as debatable historical fact in the form of a possible early outlaw community, but also because of the ambiguity with which they are perceived in the book. They are a bunch of rapacious brigands, terrorizing the entire area, but they are also held in a sort of skewed esteem because they are of legendary high birth. The clan chief, Sir Ensor, is approached by John Ridd with awe and respect, despite the fact that his own father was murdered by the Doones. And of course Lorna is not a Doone at all by birth but was abducted by them in childhood.

It is still a rattling good read. To the modern reader, Blackmore's insistent Exmoor dialect can be an irritation. Lorna herself is to be endured rather than enjoyed and one sometimes has to curb exasperation with John's self-deprecating narration. But the suspense and setting are as compelling as they must have been for its mass readership around the turn of the century. Then, it conjured up a landscape so inviting that readers flocked to enjoy the reality. Some, indeed, were disappointed and complained that the Exmoor scenery did not match up to the dramatic quality bestowed on it by Blackmore – the hills not sufficiently precipitous, the combes (which Blackmore persisted in calling glens) not as large, gloomy and fearsome as anticipated. Even Baedeker's *Handbook to Great Britain* was affected. The compiler of the 1887 edition felt constrained to write to Blackmore about the discrepancy between the actual appearance of the supposed Doone valley and the description given in the novel.

122,521

Blackmore replied: 'I romanced therein, not to mislead any other, but solely for the uses of my story.' Fair enough, I'd say.

But Blackmore's romantic and high-flown picture of Exmoor had set a standard. In the wake of *Lorna Doone* even the guidebook authors get quite carried away by the opening up of the west. A down-to-earth gazetteer of 1910, crisply informative about population numbers, early closing and market days, places of worship and the various fares from Paddington, reaches for another kind of language when advertising the scenic delights of the moor:

Withal there is green, green everywhere, a luxuriant growth rioting in colour, from the moorland to the very foot of the cliff, where the waves kiss the woods, as if here the mermaids and dryads made close alliance, and met each other on common ground amid those many brawling streams that rush over boulder and through bracken down to the sea.

The railway had reached Plymouth by 1848, though the comprehensive netting of most of the peninsula by branch lines was to continue for many years. There were of course far more significant implications than those of increased tourism. The West Country had hitherto been isolated from national life. It was also highly regional – a patchwork of definitive inward-looking localities. The railway revolution not only united the area to the rest of the country but also facilitated internal communications with all that implied for commerce and industry. In that most symbolic of all railway innovations, Greenwich Time supplanted local time. Comment in the region's newspapers expanded to include matters of national concern. Above all, alien accents were heard through Somerset down into the toe of Cornwall. The visitors had arrived.

The creation of the railway system prompted mass movement. Cheap fares, day trips, summer holidays. People began to look beyond their own immediate locality in a way never before possible. The expansion of horizons seems comparable only with that occasioned by cheap air travel in the twentieth century. Maps of nineteenth-century railway construction show those black lines creeping out from the cities to ensnare the country much as air routes net the globe today. A new landscape was created, not least in the private and particular scenery of the railway lines themselves – those isolated habitats which in summer can seem like ribbons of secret unvisited gardens winding their way the length and breadth of the country. Drifts of ox-eye daisies, banks of dog roses. Stands of lupins and rosebay willowherb. The great buddleia bushes that billow at the approach to stations. And perhaps above all that yellow flow of Oxford ragwort which seems like a herbal diaspora to match that of the liberated urban masses. Richard Mabey describes in his *Flora Britannica* how a plant was noticed in the Oxford University Botanic Gardens by Joseph Banks in the 1770s, an evident rarity, possibly raised by Linnaeus. Its seed drifted out and began to colonize the old walls of the city:

By the 1830s it had arrived at Oxford Railway Station, and from there it set off down the Great Western Railway. It found the granite chips and clinker of the permanent way a congenial substitute for its natural dry habitats in the southern European mountains, and by the end of the nineteenth century it was well-established in many southern English counties. The slipstream of trains seemed to help the seeds on their way. Now it is distributed over almost the whole of England and Wales, even down to the tip of Cornwall.

Brunel's majestic feat of engineering crept west section by section. The Great Western itself opened as far as Bristol in 1841. Beyond that the several other lines later to be absorbed into the Great Western probed further west and reached out north and south within the peninsula – the Bristol and Exeter Railway, the South Devon and Dorset, the Cornwall and West Cornwall Railway. By 1862 you could travel from London to Taunton in three and three-quarter hours (just under two today) and by 1871 you could change there on to the West Somerset Railway and proceed all the way to Minehead (impossible today). The Exmoor area was easily accessible to anyone with the tourist-class return fare from Paddington (twenty-five shillings by 1910).

The construction of the system had been a matter of mile-by-mile negotiation with landowners and others with entrenched interests. There was intense conflict between those who welcomed the railway and those who did not, those who had a shrewd understanding of all that it implied and those who shrank from innovation. West Country towns and resorts were quick to see that the arrival or otherwise of the trains meant prosperity or decline. Ilfracombe was a well-established 'bathing place' on the north coast of Devon during the mid century, but its burghers soon realized that achievement of major resort status depended on a direct line. There were even instances of violence towards the supporters of an obstructing landowner (which culminated in readings of the Riot Act) but in 1870 the Barnstaple and Ilfracombe Railway opened successfully, after which the town reigned supreme on the north Devon coast.

Minehead was faced with a similar problem. The West Somerset Railway stalked towards the town with dismaying slowness. Its initial objective was Watchet harbour, which was achieved in 1862 by way of Norton Fitzwarren, Bishops Lydeard, Crocombe, Stogumber and Williton – that lovely litany of names with which I grew familiar riding the same line in the late 1940s as a schoolgirl. Watchet was not of course a resort but a serious working port trading up and down the Bristol Channel as it had done since Saxon times – the advantages of rail access were obvious. Indeed, at this point in the middle of the century it embarked upon its period of greatest activity with the opening of the West Somerset Mineral Railway in the late 1850s – a twelve-mile inclined railway bringing iron ore from the workings on the Brendon Hills for shipment to the foundries across the channel in south Wales. The Welsh miners too were visitors, many of whom came to stay, but visitors very different from the influx brought by the railway. Minehead struggled for inclusion into the network from the 1860s on but the Minehead Railway did not finally open the eight and a quarter miles from Watchet to Minehead until 1874.

The West Somerset Railway was axed by the dreaded Dr Beeching in 1971. I remember the outcry. I recall the intense pleasure of the journey, the train slowly creaking its winding way from the metropolitan neutrality of Taunton deep into the familiar hills. I got off at Washford, travelling to Golsoncott for the school holidays. That last stretch of the return was to be savoured – release from the horrors of boarding school, a fresh appraisal of the beloved landscape. The train's shadow moved alongside, sliding across the tipping fields, topped with a trail of dark smoke puffs. Sometimes the engine ground to an unscheduled stop and sat wheezing steam while you stared in sudden intimacy at a bank of primroses a few feet beyond the window, or met the affronted gaze of a group of sheep.

The line survives today as a scenic railway, catering for

the tourist trade. Back then, it carried much local traffic – schoolchildren, shoppers bound for Taunton – as well as the long-distance visitors. In its early years, these would have had one further change to make on arrival at Minehead, if they planned to penetrate further, to Porlock or to those favoured coastal villages at the foot of the moor, Lynmouth and Lynton. They descended from the train – that triumph of nineteenth-century engineering – and climbed on to a four-in-hand coach for the final leg of the journey, moving in effect from a modern transport system back on to that of the eighteenth century. A photograph of the Lynton coach on the Minehead seafront in about 1900 shows a small vehicle topped with fourteen passengers, never mind the invisible four inside. The horses have that resigned cab-horse droop, as well they might with the one-in-four gradient of Porlock Hill ahead of them – though a contemporary photograph of a coach outside the Ship Inn at Porlock, about to set off for Lynmouth, shows what seems to be a smaller six-in-hand with fewer passengers, so maybe a further change was made at that point.

I realize with a jolt of surprise that the coaches must have been a familiar sight to the young Hewetts. They rode in them, no doubt. And this fact makes their generation suddenly very distant. For my own grandchildren, a steam train is an interesting archaism. For my grandmother, once upon a time, a coach and four was not worth a second glance; not many years later she was the owner of a Standard 8 car – a pioneer woman driver. Her experience of this interface of transport systems gives me a sharpened vision of the way in which a life spans the metamorphoses of its backdrop. The furnishings are superseded, each one tethered to its time. People too are reinvented, adjusting according to temperament and incli-nation, vaulting ahead of their day, hanging back in distaste.

The six young Hewetts would step out of their cluttered late Victorian clothes (up to a point), would assume the mind-set of the twentieth century (to a degree). But subsumed within each of them there would always be a person for whom a form of transport familiar to Samuel Johnson had been a perfectly normal sight.

Recollection cannot be shared – that fragmented vision of elsewhere with which each of us lives. In those old photographs of my young grandmother an incarnation of a person I would one day know looks out at me from elsewhere. The background scenery of Exmoor is today much as it was then, but when I pore over those groups I see them sited not in a place but a time. They invite deconstruction – I can only see them through the lens of my own curiosity. There they sit, people who are both oddly familiar and also absolute strangers; they are themselves – and a great deal more besides.

The Children on the Sampler

My grandmother was a fine needlewoman – both creative and technically accomplished. Her preferred medium was Winchester work – wool embroidery in a subtle and intricate colour spectrum. But she made excursions into other forms and one of her *chefs-d'œuvre* was the sampler that she made of Golsoncott itself in 1946, which stood as a fire-screen in the drawing room and is now the centrepiece of my study in London.

It is formal and stylized, in the sampler tradition, with the house at the top and beneath it significant elements of the garden – lily pond with goldfish shimmering beneath the blue stitched water, dovecot with white doves, sundial, mole and molehill, frog, toad, dragonfly . . . Below that is the stable block, horses peering from loose boxes, each named, and a row of prancing dogs beneath – Sheltie and Waif and Merlin and the famous Dingo, a real Australian dingo bought from London Zoo by my aunt Rachel.

At the very bottom is a line of children. Not, as you might think, grandchildren, but the wartime evacuees.

There were six of them – six children under five. Rachel went to London shortly after the outbreak of war to work for the Citizens' Advice Bureau based at Toynbee Hall in Whitechapel (then part of the London Borough of Stepney, itself now incorporated into Tower Hamlets) which served as a relief centre for those bombed out or otherwise in need of help as a result of the Blitz. In the autumn of 1940 she informed her mother that Golsoncott was now an official war nursery and that six children would shortly be arriving, along with the matron allocated for such groups of under-fives evacuated without mothers. My grandmother took it on the chin and set about reorganizing the house. The old nursery and night nursery were made over to the party, along with the attic rooms that had formerly been servants' quarters. The evacuees ate in the servants' sitting-room next to the kitchen. At night the children must have lain staring up at the night-nursery ceiling on which Margaret Tarrant fairies flew around a midnight blue sky spangled with stars. The children came from Stepney, a borough where around 200,000 people lived at an average density of twelve per dwelling. From there to Golsoncott. Confronted with this situation, I assume that they did the normal and natural thing – howled for their mothers and wet their beds. My grandmother, who didn't have to do the washing, took a kindly interest and gave them much the same treatment as grandchildren received when there were any to hand – they had the run of the garden and were summoned to the drawing-room after tea where she read to them from Beatrix Potter. She found the evacuees' Cockney accents distasteful and hoped to correct these. (By contrast, Somerset accents were considered entirely agreeable and to be respected – a neat instance of the perceived aesthetic chasm between town and country.)

Perhaps today, somewhere, there is a person of about my own age whose memory bank includes a bizarre fragment in which he or she sits on a cushion in a vast room while a benign madwoman with peculiar diction reads aloud from diminutive books. I'm not sure how long the evacuees stayed but they were certainly there for two or three years and were legendary figures by the time I returned to Golsoncott in the late forties.

Naughty and engaging Georgie of the golden curls, who climbed the cedar of Lebanon, got stuck and had to be rescued by ladder. Pert little Maureen, who once scarpered off down to the village and was found hanging around outside the Valiant Soldier. After the war, leftover money from the Anglo-American Relief Organization, which had funded several such evacuee nurseries, was used to pay for summer holidays for former evacuees. Rachel used to oversee this operation and distribute joyous leggy adolescents around the area. The evacuee experience was notoriously various – these must have been among the happier instances. One of Rachel's protégés, a girl called June, was still coming to Golsoncott for a summer stint in the late forties, by which time she was a histrionic adolescent in love with my aunt, spending her time hanging around outside Rachel's studio and the stables in the hope of a passing word. One lad originally billeted on a local farm continued to holiday in the area as the father of his own family and eventually set up as a butcher in Minehead.

Rachel acted as unofficial billeting officer in 1940, exploiting her network of local acquaintances, touring the area on horseback to target farms and cottages and allocate Toynbee Hall children. It is the role seized on by Basil Seal in Evelyn Waugh's *Put Out More Flags*, foisting the fearful Connolly family upon carefully selected genteel victims, the more frail and addicted to gracious living, the better. Basil's motivation is pecuniary and gleefully malicious. In Rachel's case her war work fired her social conscience. But west Somerset was not to know that and she may well have caused a certain consternation, trotting briskly into farmyards, smiling sweetly and talking not of the next meet but of numbers of bedrooms and sanitary facilities.

Rachel was one of the many for whom sudden exposure

to the realities of pre-war urban poverty changed an entire perception of their society. She was in her thirties and had lived all her life in the country, her time divided between riding and hunting and her career as a talented wood engraver and avant-garde painter and sculptor. London was simply a place you visited for social or cultural reasons. For her, as for most middle-class people, the teeming tracts of the East End were nothing but names on a map, Stepney, Bow, East Ham, Poplar. They were invisible and inconceivable. Then came 1940. Rachel saw – many saw – and their perception of society would never be quite the same again. The circumstances in which hundreds of thousands of children were growing up – the malnutrition, the absence of home hygiene – shocked even those who should have known. Neville Chamberlain wrote to his wife: 'I never knew that such conditions existed, and I feel ashamed of having been so ignorant of my neighbours.'

The revelation for rural middle-class England created by that diaspora of the Blitz evacuees was to contribute to pressure for the social reforms of the post-war period. The effects on people who experienced the evacuation trauma were powerful. The two nations – rural and urban, prosperous and poor – met face to face in a way that had not happened before; indeed many of the hosts and evacuees lived under the same roof for months or years. Rachel worked in Stepney with bombed-out families throughout 1940 and 1941; she saw at first hand how these people lived, how they had been living throughout her own tranquil and cushioned youth at Golsoncott. In 1945 she voted Labour, and continued to do so for the rest of her life. My grandmother, whose own form of paternal Toryism remained unshaken, learned to live with this. Locally, Rachel's politics were seen as an artistic eccentricity, but something you did not tangle with.

The extent of the dismay and perplexity engendered by the evacuees suggests that there was no such thing as pre-war rural poverty. Of course there was – but it was different. The very tag given to the evacuee children – the 'skinnies' – evokes the distinction. Rural children ate better; however low agricultural wages were, there was always the extra resource of the cottage garden. Rural working-class life was hard, cottages were damp and cold, but the poverty was qualitatively different from urban poverty. The countryside was deeply disturbed by what it now saw.

A report on urban conditions published in 1943 estimated that up to 30 per cent of children were living in a situation of dire poverty. Hosts of evacuees found themselves coping with children who were sewn into their only set of clothes and whose only shoes were a pair of plimsolls, children with scabies and nits, children who were visibly undernourished. Many, of course, were not in such a condition – inevitably it was the extreme cases that attracted comment and attention. My aunt, preparing her mother for the arrival of the Golsoncott allocation, wrote briskly: 'They will have doctor's certificates, but will need pretty thorough baths. Do you mind? . . . I think you had better get toothbrushes, combs etc. as even if the children bring them they may not be too clean.' Many evacuee children came from homes in which there was no bath, where they customarily slept on the floor and ate meals in the street – a slice of bread and marge in hand. Their rural hosts were frequently a notch or more up the social ladder; the bewildered children found that the country was a place where things were done differently.

The mass movement of mothers and children in the war years produced two different kinds of confrontation. Firstly, there was the apposition of country and city, an ancient divide, but one of which many had become ignorant or oblivious. Peering back into the 1940s, it is difficult to realize how deeply polarized that society was then – even for one who was around at the time and exposed to its stringent rules and assumptions. There is a fair amount of mutual ignorance today between city and country, but it is tempered by two powerful forces of enlightenment – television and general mobility. The sight, sound and function of the countryside are familiar to all, if only through the windows of a car or as the backdrop to some news item or rural drama series. There cannot today be many children who are surprised to find that a cow is bigger than a dog – as were some evacuees who had only ever seen such creatures in pictures. Equally, a Somerset farm labourer today may never have visited London or Manchester but the inner-city scene is a presence in any living-room; everyone has stared at Toxteth, at cardboard city on the South Bank, at human bundles stretched out in shop doorways, at grid-locked streets shimmering with exhaust fumes.

There was also the heightened class confrontation, with the newly sharpened perception everywhere that there were others whose lifestyle was startling and provocative. There were different apprehensions of the class divide in the country and in the cities. In rural areas rich and poor were used to living in proximity to each other – the local big house was visible, its occupants known by sight and by name. The face of patronage was one that could be recognized. This cannot have made the chasm any more acceptable, but it was an economic landscape that was familiar and in that sense one that was domesticated. For the residents of Stepney or Bow, the nobs in the West End were a distant phenomenon in newspapers or newsreels. Just as many East Enders' only knowledge of the country came from their annual hop-picking excursions, so their experience of the upper classes was indirect and indistinct. The prosperity of country gentry came as a revelation, seen up close with all the telling details of a lifestyle that must have seemed barely credible.

The evacuation exercises involved around 4 million people, and that is just the quantity of actual evacuees. Add to this number all the host families, the officials responsible in the reception areas, people like my aunt who became involved in war work, and one sees that a vast swathe of the nation was affected.

There were three main waves of evacuation. The first – and in many ways the most traumatic and astonishing – was that of 1–3 September 1939, when 1,473,000 people were moved from Britain's cities, the majority of them before war was declared on the morning of 3 September. The next phase was the so-called 'trickle' evacuation once the bombing had started, when around 1,550,000 were moved to the reception areas between September 1940 and the end of 1941. Finally, a third wave of a million people fled the cities again in 1944 in response to the summer of the flying bombs. There were mothers, pregnant women, the old and the sick among these huge migrations, but the vast majority were children. By the end of the Blitz, only 7,736 children had been killed as a result of bombing. Only? But it would have been many more, without the evacuations. Some 60,000 adults died, half of them in London alone, with a further 86,000 seriously injured.

The statistics are dizzying, but they are also meaningless until you think of them in terms of lived experience, as conveyed in the dry but telling prose of Richard Titmuss, official historian of the evacuation exercise: 'From the first day of September 1939 evacuation ceased to be a problem of administrative planning. It became instead a multitude of problems in human relationships.' The Golsoncott infants were so young that their time there should have been subsumed for the most part into the murk of their very early years. But they had been separated from their mothers, with all that implies. Between 30,000 and 40,000 under-fives met this fate, and even at the time developmental psychologists were expressing unease at this trauma and its potential long-term effects. For older children, the stark experience of being swept away from their homes and dumped down among strangers would have been mitigated only by childhood's absence of solid assumptions and expectations. Children exist in a continuous present and make no presumptions about the future. They know already that the world is a startling and unreliable place, where anything is apparently possible and in which you are required to conform to mysterious codes imposed by the adult world. Every child picks its way through a complex minefield of requirements, learning self-preservation as it goes. This natural flexibility of children must have enabled most of them to respond more expediently to the situation than an adult could. And indeed the reaction of so many accompanying mothers is an indication of this – the vast majority of those evacuated in the first wave beat it back to the cities before the end of 1939 when it became apparent that the bombs were not yet falling.

But the children could make no such choice. The abundant literature of evacuation preserves their perplexity, resentment, anguish . . . and sometimes their pleasure, surprise and curiosity. The situation must have seemed part and parcel of an always unpredictable world, and they reacted according to temperament and in the light of their particular circumstances, with many demonstrating a robust adaptability. Their voices ring out over the years – those children of the 1940s who were part of an unprecedented diaspora intended to save their lives, but which would also end up as the unanticipated instrument of social enlightenment.

The inner-city children were confronted with alien practices. Their hosts were from a wider social range. Compulsory billeting took no account of social status – in theory, at least – but simply looked at numbers of rooms and sanitary facilities available in a home. The measure of surplus accommodation was one person per habitable room, which, according to pre-war assessments would give a reassuring 4.8 million billets. When it came to the crunch, things were not quite so straightforward. The nation's potential hosts seem to have divided into those who saw it as their patriotic duty to provide hospitality and those who were determined to resist at all costs. Not surprisingly, resistance grew stronger higher up the social scale. The 1939 wave of evacuation had tested the waters. Its effect was to make billeting far more difficult the second time round. By late 1940, a Ministry of Health senior officer could say grimly: 'The real hard core is the upper middle classes' (at this point I think fondly of my grandmother). There were of course various categories granting exemption – age and infirmity, chronic illness, war work and so forth. Billeting officers described the blizzard of medical certificates provided by compliant doctors. And of course the billeting officers themselves, appointed by the local authorities, became objects of fear and suspicion.

But it was indeed a lot to ask of people – an invasion of their homes and their privacy, a disruption of their lives. Titmuss nicely nails the matter once again: 'For the authorities to impose – and to maintain for five years – a policy of billeting in private homes was a severe test of human nature.' And human nature responded in all its infinite variety. But the

squeamish reaction of some middle-class hosts was not the
only reason why the evacuees were billeted for the most
part with poorer families. The tactfully phrased plea of one
evacuated mother says a lot: 'I can't eat like them; although
it's kind I'd give anything to be put with my own class.'

Unaccompanied children could not recognize the problem
as one of culture clash. Like all children, they knew what was
normal and what was not, and reacted accordingly. One child
commented: 'The country is a funny place. They never tell
you you can't have no more to eat, and under the bed is
wasted.' Two little boys from Glasgow, confronted with a
white-sheeted bed, recoiled in horror: 'That's a bed for dead
folk.' Sleeping and eating habits were often matters of conflict.
The survey compiled in September 1940 by the National Federation of Women's Institutes provides revealing evidence not
just on the condition and assumptions of evacuees but also
on the attitudes of the usually well-meaning but frequently
horrified hostesses. Bed-wetting and head lice were a constant
refrain (more later on these seminal matters). But the problem
of eating habits ran them close. Countrywomen were dis-
mayed at the city child's habit of demanding a slice of bread
and marge or dripping (a luxury) to eat in the street or on the
doorstep. Many evacuees could be persuaded to sit at a table
only with difficulty. The children, for their part, were suspicious of fruit, green vegetables and what the country
regarded as 'a plain cooked meal'. They were used to fish and
chips, cakes, bread and jam. Evacuee and host eyed one
another across an abyss.

The Golsoncott evacuees arrived in December 1940. Rachel
wrote in advance to her mother:

The two whom I know are certainties are Raymond Margries and George Marling, both aged three. I forget what they look like, but the parents of George are very decent people, the Margries are all right too. Miss James (Matron) . . . will bring them down.'

Shortly after, she wrote again:

Beside George and Raymond, there is now Joyce Owen, aged three. She comes from a very poor home indeed, nothing could be worse. I was sorry to have her, but she is a Stepney child, and I could not refuse. Maureen Sullivan, four, may be coming, and Brenda Durman, three, is another possibility. The sixth will be from another district and a girl . . .

Poor little Joyce Owen. The 'very poor home' may account for her being evacuated alone, so young. One wonders why particular families were willing – or more probably obliged – to send very small children off without their mothers. And inevitably one suspects that poverty, large numbers of children and impossible home circumstances must have been at the back of it in many cases. Mothers in dire circumstances with large families would have been more inclined to part with an infant. Perhaps Joyce's mother was in the sort of situation highlighted by Margery Spring Rice's 1939 Pelican, *Working-Class Wives, Their Health and Conditions* (which itself induces intense nostalgia for that high-minded, eclectic, enquiring and infinitely useful blue-spined imprint – publishing has never been the same since).

A woman such as Joyce's mother may well have had too many children because advice on birth control was not readily available. She was very likely anaemic – out of a sample of 1,250 women questioned by the Women's Health Enquiry

Committee of 1933, 558 had been diagnosed as anaemic – and those were only the ones who had had the problem diagnosed by a doctor. Anyone who has been temporarily anaemic knows what it feels like – continuous lassitude, being out of breath if you climb stairs or walk uphill, permanent fatigue. Before the war, huge numbers of working-class women felt like that all the time. Joyce's mother may also have suffered from headaches, constipation and haemorrhoids, rheumatism, carious teeth, gynaecological problems, varicose veins, ulcerated legs, phlebitis – conditions all found to have a high incidence among this sample of women. She was lucky if she sat down for half an hour between rising at 6.30 a.m. and winding up the day at around 9 p.m. The Spring Rice account is a dispassionate survey of the condition of such women, concluding that the factors contributing to the dismal picture were poverty, ill health and a lack of trained knowledge on the part of the women. The book anticipated post-war welfare reforms by advocating such things as Family Allowances to be paid to the mother and an extension of the National Health Insurance system to cover the wives and children of insured men.

The Golsoncott evacuees were a part of the second and extended 'trickle' evacuation of 1940. By the time they arrived at their safe haven London was burning. My aunt's letters home from September of that year onwards are a vivid account of what it was like to work in the East End throughout the worst of the Blitz. Her main task at Toynbee Hall at that point was to cope with the increasing flow of families who had been bombed out or who had become so demoralized that they wanted to be evacuated. But by then the pressures on the reception areas were such that billets were hard to find, and she was frequently having to tell distraught mothers that nothing could be done unless and until they were actually homeless. She rails against the apparent inefficiency of the Stepney authorities:

The people there really are wonderful. Lots were wandering, homeless, towards the City this morning, with suitcases, all they had saved: but they seemed quite resigned and unmoved . . . the arrangements for the homeless really are very bad in Stepney – it is a disgrace. In Bermondsey, where hardly a street is unbombed, I believe it is far better. None of the homeless people I had in were grumbling; they were all determined we must stick it out . . . The Mayor of Stepney spoke on the 6 p.m. news last night; I don't suppose you heard him but, luckily, I did. He said he was giving out money to anyone needing it, so I shall send him all the hard cases I have in next week with a note asking him to give them rail tickets etc.

Rachel was thirty-two – energetic, resourceful and with a streak of adventurousness. She seized on this wartime experience – quite alien to anything she had ever known. Sometimes a note of exhilaration creeps into her descriptions of London in 1940:

We had a marvellous view of an air fight so high up that nothing but the extraordinary patterns of the frozen exhausts could be seen. These stayed for ages, half an hour at least, after the planes had gone by, so that soon the sky was full of circles and strange patterns. Sometimes the three German planes, which could be distinguished by their close formation, which left three exhaust tracks tight together, were flying exactly into the tail of their own track. It all seems like slow motion – you see our fighters coming in at an angle to attack, but so slowly, apparently, that you can tell before if they will be in time to attack or not.

In her off-duty moments, she went into the recently Blitzed areas and sketched, thus accumulating a bank of background material for her sequence of powerful oil paintings and engravings of bombed buildings. These are among her most arresting and innovative work; just as exposure to the social realities of working-class London sharpened her political awareness, so the ruined and dramatic landscape created by the Blitz seems to have given a new intensity and energy to her paintings and engravings. Chimneys stand stark against smoky skies, iron girders twist and rear, interior walls of floorless buildings bear the ghostly exuberance of an overmantel, the flourish of a cornice, a patch of patterned wallpaper. Unfazed by a situation that changed with each night's wave of bombers, she drove to and from Stepney each day:

Last night, driving back through the City, it was most exciting. A policeman told me it was impossible [to drive], but luckily I knew a way from coming through in the morning. We bumped over fire hoses all the way and passed rows and rows of engines and pumps. Every here and there the firemen silently playing their hoses on smouldering buildings – all in the dark, of course.

By this time in 1940 many people were only too anxious to leave London, and even more desperate to get their children out. As other cities too were targeted, the demand for evacuation spread and the matter of finding billets became more and more urgent. It was also considerably more problematic. The country was now wise to what might lie in store; the inclination to perform a patriotic duty was more often tempered with a sense of self-preservation. But the authorities had learned some lessons from the chaotic scenes of the September 1939 evacuation. There would be no more unstructured mass exits, with parties of children simply herded on to the next train, regardless of destination; no more of those pathetic scenes in church and village halls, with labelled children awaiting selection by some host, 'scenes reminiscent of a cross between an early Roman slave market and Selfridges bargain basement . . .' (in the much-quoted words of the deputy evacuation officer to the West Hartlepool Local Education Authority).

On 3 September 1939 I was at Golsoncott, aged six, visiting England – a place I did not know and would barely remember – for the last time until 1945. I would shortly return to Egypt, where I had been born and would spent the rest of my childhood, caught up in a different theatre of the war. Sitting on the carpet in the Golsoncott drawing-room, I heard a thin dry man's voice coming from the wireless and wondered why we all had to sit in silence and why everyone looked so solemn.

At Williton station, four miles away, the war had begun two days before. Four hundred schoolchildren and their teachers arrived, allocated to the Watchet area; a similar number went to Minehead. On the next day, Saturday 2 September, the Williton Rural District Council reception party stood ready for 800 of an agreed allocation of 2,000 London schoolchildren. Billets had already been found, in Williton itself and the surrounding area. Local district officers had worked hard during the summer – as had their colleagues all over the country – responding to the government directives in anticipation of intensive bombing of London as soon as war broke out. They knew where they were going to put every single one of those children.

When the train arrived at 3.30 p.m. it carried a load of passengers somewhat different from that expected: 700 mothers with babies and toddlers, plus pregnant women.

Heroically, the Williton officials and their helpers set to and somehow found accommodation for everyone before midnight – a whole swathe of new billets. They dared not use up the original ones lest the trainload of children and teachers awaited should turn up after all. It never did, but on the Monday another 770 mothers and children arrived. Within three days the district's population had increased by 1,500.

The chaos of that three-day evacuation exodus stemmed from the fact that while preparations had been dutifully carried out in the so-called reception areas in earmarking billets, not enough thought had been given to the logistics of moving such large numbers by train with such rapidity out of the cities. This accounts for the intense complications over which contingents of evacuees were to go to which destination. There were indeed plans and arrangements, but in the event the parties of children, and of mothers and children, arrived at the main London stations from their various gathering points in such a continuous stream and in such numbers that they had to be marshalled on to the first available train, regardless of where it was going or who it was expecting to take, before the station reached saturation point.

Hence the confusion so vividly recalled in later life by both the adults and children involved. The platforms packed with little figures slung about with gas masks, cardboard suitcases, brown paper parcels. The interminable journeys without sustenance or lavatories; the late-night arrivals at some unknown destination where sharp-eyed hosts waited to pounce on the least unappealing-looking evacuees. Curiously, many of the children recalled an atmosphere of excitement and expectation, though for most this soon evaporated as they confronted the reality of exile with strangers. For the adults concerned those three hectic days in September 1939 and their aftermath must have been very different. Teachers had to try to cope with stressed, unruly and disorientated charges under difficult circumstances – frequently there were no adequate classroom facilities available at the reception destination, or they had to accept the grudging hospitality of local schools and share premises on a rota basis. Parents had to say goodbye without knowing how or when they would see their children again. Visiting was of course possible, and government subsidy was available for those unable to find the cost of rail fares – but in wartime conditions travel was difficult, and many of the children had been sent far from their homes.

Above all, there was the grim prospect of imminent attack, fostered by the precipitate nature of the evacuation exercise. Many people must have had an icy knot of fear in their stomachs. Anyone alive to official anticipation of what would probably happen in the first few days and weeks of war would have been expecting the end of the world that they knew. Since the early 1930s there had been a standing assessment of the potential damage from aerial bombardments in the event of the war with Germany, based on what was known of German rearmament and also on the extent of raids at the end of the First World War. It was considered that an initial mass bombardment of London and the south-east could result in 3,500 tons of high explosive falling on London in the first twenty-four hours, followed by 700 tons a day during the ensuing two weeks. The consequence would be an immediate exodus of 3 to 4 million people. The evacuation plans drawn up in the years before the war in anticipation of this outcome were not only to save lives; they were also intended to pre-empt the mass panic and consequent breakdown of law and order that would be one of the enemy's main objectives in such a bombardment.

It was considered that this initial attack could result in 600,000 civilian deaths, with twice that number of injuries. One person in twenty-five would be a casualty, with more in London itself. Such a prediction sounds like the Armageddon scenario of nuclear war; in that light the discovery by Mass-Observation researchers that numbers of Britons contemplated killing their families if war broke out is not perhaps too startling. And as a constant reminder of the chilling and unpredictable future there were the grim accessories – the sandbags banked against buildings, the blackout regulations, the gas masks.

Those gas masks. If anything is the potent symbol of evacuation, it is those dumpy little boxes hanging from every child. I had one myself, briefly, and remember its mysterious and worrying significance; I did not understand what it was, except that I must not lose it or I would die. It was my personal baggage on the flight across Europe in September 1939 to join my parents in Egypt. I think I did lose it, in Venice, and was soundly berated, but without it everything seemed less threatening.

In the event, of course, the 38 million gas masks issued in Britain were never needed. And the pre-war calculations of casualty levels, founded on incorrect assumptions based on the effects of bombing in 1917–18, proved to be considerable overestimates. The estimate of fifty casualties per ton of high explosive dropped turned out to be more in the region of fifteen to twenty. The total figures of those killed and injured up and down the country during the Blitz are sobering enough, but they were nothing like what had been feared.

But it was chilling expectations that prompted the whole evacuation scheme. In such a climate the confusion of the September 1939 evacuation is entirely understandable. And then nothing happened – no bombs, just a few false alarms which set the sirens wailing as a sinister taster of what would come eventually. Down in rural areas, the sense of anticlimax must have exacerbated the grievances of those who had taken in evacuees. Since life was going on as normal in the cities, the spirit of willing sacrifice in order to save the nation's children gave way to one of irritation and dismay at the inconvenience of harbouring cuckoos in the nest.

There was a wide range of perceived difficulties. Eating and sleeping habits, behavioural problems, inadequate clothing, the insufficiency of the government subsidy for feeding evacuees (10s. 6d. per week for the first child, 8s. 6d. per head for further children). But the dominating grievances were nits and bed-wetting.

The nits problem raises a couple of interesting and baffling questions. There was widespread infestation by head lice among the evacuees from the cities – the figures served up by the indomitable National Federation of Women's Institutes 1940 survey show variations from place to place and group to group, but it is clear that a high proportion of city children were affected and, moreover, that their parents regarded this as a normal and inevitable inconvenience. But receiving country households were appalled and shocked. The implication seems to be that country children did not have nits. Why not? They, too, lived frequently in overcrowded and insanitary conditions; they, too, went to school. The head louse moves from one host to another – when children put their heads together over a desk or in play.

Nits were a social stigma, back then. Hence, I suppose, the tight-lipped dismay of the country hostesses, especially given the apparent nitlessness of country schools and homes. Today, things are rather different. The nit is ubiquitous. My four grandchildren have all had nits at some point; most children do nowadays, so far as I can make out. This is the second puzzle: why is the post-war louse no longer confined to an urban working-class environment? Are contemporary nits more socially mobile and widespread because they are of a different strain, or is there some other factor? Whatever the explanation, an interesting footnote to cultural change over the last fifty years is the fact that the head louse is no longer a social indicator.

In the autumn of 1939, the landscape was adorned with lines of drying bedsheets. There was a prolonged spell of unseasonably warm weather, fortunately. The problem of incontinence was the one that most perturbed those on whom the evacuees were billeted, and one can entirely see why – a nuisance at any time, a major challenge when without benefit of washing machines or central heating. And the problem was frequent, giving rise to much comment about dirty habits and inadequate toilet training. But there is a fine and correct distinction between bed-wetting, which is precisely that, and enuresis, which is what most of the offending evacuees suffered from. Enuresis is failure to control urination and 'is an expression of mental protest. It is primarily a symptom of mental disturbance' (Titmuss again – tersely accurate). In fact, there was plenty of recognition at the time that the evacuees' nocturnal lapses were due to distress, and the fact that in most cases enuresis ceased after a few weeks or months was a reassurance. But the concerned discussion of the difficulty both at the time and since is one of the instances when the historical record vividly reflects personal experience. Behind those figures and those analyses lie the individual traumas of hundreds of thousands of children, sleeping in strange beds and inadvertently protesting.

For the adults involved, the single most significant effect of the evacuation experience was a sweeping revision of the way in which they saw their country. For city-dwellers it was an eye-opener about how the other half lived, in every sense. Of those in intimate contact with the evacuees – hosts, officials – many saw the experience as 'a dreadful lesson', recognizing that the blame for the conditions from which so many had come must be laid at the door of the nation as a whole for allowing such deprivation.

But what of the children's wider experience? Evacuation was a notoriously polarized experience and it is dangerous to generalize; for some children it was an ordeal, but for many there was much that was positive. Many were received with warmth, grew attached to their foster parents and benefited from the opportunities offered. My husband Jack was one such fortunate evacuee. He and his brother Jim, aged ten and eight, were evacuated from a council estate in Newcastle-on-Tyne to the Cumbrian village of Maulds Mayburn. They were billeted on a farm – the sort of Lake District hill farm which in those days had changed little in 500 years. No electricity, no running water. The boys' previous experience of life beyond Newcastle had been restricted to brief summer stints in a caravan in Whitley Bay. Now, they found themselves caught up in the life of a working farm, where everyone was expected to turn to and help. Jack remembered helping to harness horses, carrying hot mash out to the hens on sharp winter mornings, haymaking, lambing. He remembered the killing of the pig and the side of bacon which hung all winter from a beam in the kitchen. He remembered exulting over the first fall of snow; the farmer, for whom snow was not good news, grimly sent him out into the yard and made him stay there till he understood what it implied. He remembered the integrated life of the hamlet, in which everyone farmed or was otherwise dependent upon a local economy. A few years ago, we visited Maulds Mayburn. The cottages and farmhouses were in spanking condition, outside each stood a Volvo or a Saab. It had become a weekenders' village.

His evacuee experience gave Jack a lifelong affinity with the country. More than that, it provided opportunity. The farmer's wife had been a schoolteacher. Helping Jack with homework brought back from the village school (which incorporated all the children in the area, aged from five to fifteen), she realized that he was a very bright little boy. She set about coaching him for entrance to Newcastle Grammar School, which itself had been evacuated to Penrith. He got in, and thus was propelled in the direction of Cambridge and his subsequent life as an academic.

Maulds Mayburn and Golsoncott in 1940 were both backwaters in which nothing happened except the routines of daily life, the cycle of the year. A farming community; a country house. Both seem like places exempt from the dictation of public events. They were not, of course – nowhere is. The war directed Jack and his brother to that farm, and when I look at my grandmother's sampler I can no longer see it as a conventional celebration of domestic certainties, knowing what I know. Once decoded, those small stitched figures seem to shimmer with significance. They are as formal and ordered as the rest of the sampler, which is itself faithful to the unchanging requirements of such pieces of work – it is in precise descent from its antecedents of the eighteenth and nineteenth centuries, down to the stitches used and the disposition of important features. But the children are an element of meaningful disorder, when you know who they are. The turbulence of the twentieth century has invaded the quiet and private life of the sampler.

The Gong Stand, The Book of Common Prayer *and the Potted-Meat Jars*

The gong was in the hall, beside the vestibule door. The large brass disc was suspended within a wooden stand, surmounted by a ledge and with the felt-headed striker hanging from a hook. Time was, it was sounded to warn the family that a meal was about to be served – an imperious crescendo that would have been audible throughout the house. In my adolescence, it was seldom used and seemed to be a symbol of vanished rituals. By then, the pre-war posse of 'staff' was already mythical. The cook, the parlourmaid, the housemaids, the gardeners, the grooms. From time to time, when the going was good, there was a resident couple – the wife doing the cooking, the husband laying tables, lighting fires, stoking the boiler. He would also strike the gong, but with a diffident hand, as though recognizing that this was barely appropriate under the circumstances.

The ledge that formed the top of the stand was still useful. Incoming mail was placed on it, and also letters to be posted. When my grandmother and aunt came down to breakfast on Sundays they put their copies of *The Book of Common Prayer* and their hymnals on the gong stand. I can see them now – the two neat stacks imbuing the morning with difference, and significance.

The potted-meat jars were kept in a box in the scullery cupboard. They too were symbolic of ritual. They came out at Easter, and at Easter only.

At Easter, at Christmas and at Harvest Festival the church

had to be decorated. Harvest Festival passed me by – I would have been at boarding school. But the Easter and Christmas decorating rituals are like iron in the soul, to this day. The ice-cold church. The sodden ropes of ivy. The venomous branches of holly. The dripping flowers, the cavalcade of vases and pots and jugs. The potted-meat jars, above all.

The church is at Rodhuish, the small hamlet down the hill from Golsoncott. The little whitewashed chapel of St Bartholomew, built around 1250, is one of the smallest churches in the west of England. Its seven pews on either side of the aisle seat a congregation of sixty or so, with room for a few more in the gallery at the back, itself a relic of days when the music accompanying services was supplied by a local band. In the late 1940s there was an organ, out of tune, played by a local amateur and causing some distress to my grandmother, who was musical. The congregation could reach capacity at religious festivals, but for the rest of the year there was just the hard core of a dozen or so.

There was a rota of flower arrangers for ordinary Sundays, but the major festivals were traditionally my grandmother's preserve. When I was fourteen I was allocated the potted-meat jars. No doubt it was seen as a privilege and a mark of maturity. The pulpit was the feature in question: what you had to do was set each jar against one of the upright bits of its woodwork, pass a length of raffia twine behind and attempt to knot this around the slippery neck of the glass jar. Eastertime seems always to have been bitterly chill; the raffia defied cold fingers, the jars lurched from side to side. After an hour or two of this endeavour you at last had the pulpit studded all over with jars which you then filled with water to serve as containers for primroses, scillas and jonquils. The whole structure was then carefully masked by a shroud of ivy from which the flowers rose, miraculously fresh. It was my grandmother's *pièce de résistance.*

Christmas was differently arduous, and even more uncomfortable. The temperature within the church was lower than that outside – shedding coat, scarf or gloves would have been out of the question. You were already chilled to the bone from foraging in the Golsoncott garden for ivy, holly and other greenery. This huge wet mass was then piled into the back of Rachel's Land-Rover to be taken to the church and hauled inside, soaking yourself and the church floor in the process. Every window-sill had to be swathed; likewise the font, the ends of the pews, and the pulpit again. Stabbed by holly and tripped by ivy, I endured a seasonal martyrdom, spurred on by my grandmother's exhortations but not sharing her commitment. For her, this embellishment of the little church seemed to have a significance far beyond the actual effect. I can remember her stubbornly insisting on doing it in the midst of a bout of flu.

Certainly, the ritual of church decoration must be a deeply atavistic one. The hefty use of foliage in the Rodhuish ceremonial smacks to me most interestingly of tree-worship. Holly. Ivy. Admittedly the attraction of both for decorative purposes is that they are evergreen. And they are of course the stuff of carols. But both plants are also freighted with myth, especially ivy, which is sacred to Osiris, who is a tree-spirit and a god of vegetation, and to Dionysus, also associated with tree-worship, but perhaps above all to the god Attis. He was believed to die and be resurrected in spring; this belief was commemorated in a gruesome festival where frenzied followers of his cult emasculated themselves, the god having done the same under a pine and been returned to life in the form of the tree. The cult of Attis in Roman times had ornate and complex rites, all to do with slaughter, blood, rebirth and so forth. It is impossible not to see the Christian Easter rites as an echo of those earlier ones. The ropes of ivy hauled in the Land-Rover to the church from the Golsoncott garden take on a murky and immemorial symbolism.

We sat in the second pew from the front on the left of the aisle. Always. It would have been unthinkable to sit elsewhere; equally unthinkable for anyone else to invade that pew. And all other regular attenders sat too in their established places. The farmer's wife, Mrs Thomas, sat centre-right with her daughters and small son; an old lady from one of the cottages front-right; an elderly couple back-left. Certain pews were always empty. How an unwary casual visitor would have coped with this unswerving customary occupancy, goodness knows.

For customary it was, and surely an echo of the ubiquitous earlier practice whereby church seating not only reflected the social structures of the parish but tethered each house to a particular pew or 'kneeling'. Those parishioners who moved house or left the area relinquished their right to an established position in the church each Sunday. And where you sat indicated your status – gentry at the front, yeomen and husbandmen in the middle, cottagers at the rear. Richard Gough's *The History of Myddle* (written around 1700) uses the seating plan of his parish church a few miles north of Shrewsbury to give a vivid and discursive account of an entire community in the late seventeenth century, family by family, person by person. Who was married to whom, who lived where and bequeathed what, who was 'pilfering, thievish', who 'went dayly to the alehouse', who 'lived very high and kept a pack of beagles'. The church layout becomes in effect a mnemonic system. Gough plots the occupancy of the pews and enters names and locations into each: 'Mr Ackerley for servants', 'Sleap Hall', 'Watsons tent [tenement], Davis Cottage, Baxters Cottages, Chidlows Cottage'. And the names and places become prompts – from them stream sharp vignettes of neighbours and acquaintances, what they were like and what they did, the army of people that inhabited his memory and who could be conjured up by a simple survey of the interior of the parish church.

Richard Gough's was a society in which everyone knew everyone else, and a strange face was startling. Everyone was also familiar with everyone else in Rodhuish in the late 1940s, but few people in this country today know the experience of being amazed by the presence of strangers. Gough was an educated man and a local historian, but the zest and relish with which he records those he remembers is that of an inspired gossip – one intimately involved with a community and appreciative of human foibles. However, what is most striking today about his resurrection of a vanished world is the way in which each home, each household, each person is linked to the parish church. Not only were the climactic moments of every parishioner's life stored there – baptism, marriage, burial – but where they sat on Sunday nailed them for who and what they were.

St Bartholomew's in Rodhuish is not the parish church. That is Old Cleeve, a few miles away. Generations of local residents are recorded and buried there, as are my own grandparents and aunt. But today many local people will seldom, if ever, set foot in it and their births, marriages and deaths will not be noted there. The majority of the population has floated free of the established churches and a local connection with them. Around 1700, when Richard Gough was writing, pretty well everyone would have shown up in the local church of a

Sunday. At Rodhuish today, there are about eight people who sustain St Bartholomew's by attending services and struggling to raise sufficient funds to pay the quota and keep the building running. Most of them are grey-headed. Its very survival as a functioning church is threatened.

I am an agnostic. I came out as such at around fifteen and faced up to my grandmother. In mitigation of my position I went through the Ten Commandments with her to demonstrate that I still subscribed to much the same moral code as she did – I believed it was profoundly wrong to kill people or to steal, and wrong to tell lies unless under exceptional circumstances. I believed you should honour your father and your mother, but with a few reservations. On the whole I passed on the question of coveting thy neighbour's wife and all that because surely the point was to legislate with regard to actions rather than emotions, which you couldn't do much about. And on the question of blasphemy we would have to differ. My grandmother took this pretty well through she wasn't very happy about it, but she was more flexible in some of her attitudes than one might have expected and never held this dereliction against me.

Politics were another matter. There, it was simply a matter of common sense, as far as my grandmother was concerned. She would listen kindly to my sanctimonious spiels about equality of opportunity and social injustice, with a half-smile on her face. She wouldn't have known the expression 'wet behind the ears', but that was what she was thinking. So the child proposes to vote Labour when she's twenty-one, does she? When I had finished she would eye me and produce her trump card: 'That's all very well, my dear, but who, may I ask, are then going to be the hewers of wood and drawers of water?' Back to the Authorized Version.

She was an old Tory. The Toryism of *noblesse oblige* – not in an aristocratic sense, because she wasn't that, but simply on account of a belief that to them that hath there is a certain obligation of redistribution. She was involved with a swathe of charities, with the village hall and the church. It went beyond mere financial subsidy – there was an obligation to play a part in local life, to know everybody, to take an interest in and have an opinion on local issues. Patronizing, patrician and no way to run a country – but to my mind a cut above some of the versions of conservatism we've seen since. And the role and function of the Church of England was central to her priorities and concerns. She was a paid-up Christian, but church attendance implied more than mere spiritual solace; to her, support of the church was support of the social structure. In that sense she was still a late Victorian, I suppose.

And now, in the year 2000, her agnostic granddaughter finds herself contemplating with dismay the prospect of Rodhuish church being perhaps sold off by the Church of England. Closed down. De-frocked. Reinvented as a weekend cottage, maybe. It could very well happen. I am not often able to attend a service there these days, but do so whenever possible. An ambiguous position and perhaps hypocritical to some; I myself see it as confused, but defensible on grounds of emotional commitment, if not intellectual clarity. I am there not to worship but to honour this ancient and significant little building and to acknowledge what it commemorates – the centuries of Christian dominance with all that they imply, from religious persecution to the creation of the Lindisfarne Gospels.

In 1958 there were already 370 redundant Church of England churches. Between then and 1990 a further 1,261 were made redundant, leaving some 16,000 functioning churches. These figures do not of course take into account the Nonconformist places of worship which have also fallen into disuse. A church or chapel you see today may no longer be used as such – it may be an antiques centre, a warehouse, a hall available for hire, a shopping complex or an office. It may have been given the full creative architectural going-over and reinvented as a private house. Or it may be clinging to life in the hands of the Churches Conservation Trust, to be preserved on heritage grounds and given the occasional treat of a specially contrived service. There is an elaborate mechanism for the processing of threatened churches, set up by the Church Commissioners in 1968, after a report on the problem of galloping church redundancy made clear the need for a consistent policy and strategy. The Redundant Churches Fund (now the Churches Conservation Trust) was created, charged with looking after those churches selected for preservation, the costs to be shared between Church and State, with the State providing the lion's share. Between 1969 and 1989, only just over 20 per cent of churches declared redundant ended up in the benign hands of the Redundant Churches Fund. Of the rest, 55 per cent were reinvented as antiques centres, etc., and 24 per cent were laid to eternal rest by bulldozers.

The large majority of churches within those two last categories will have been Victorian, nineteenth-century inner-city churches, or churches originally servicing the first suburban expansions. Not listed buildings, not considered heritage material except by a few fervent defenders. By and large, the bulldozers do not move in on little country churches, where even those no longer making use of them would be outraged by the destruction of an apparently immemorial landmark. Rodhuish is probably safe from that threat. Its fate, if it comes to that, will be in the hands of the Church Commissioners.

The property page of a weekend newspaper serves up timely examples of four converted churches. All appear to be nineteenth-century. A handsome late Victorian building with campanile in south London is now 'six stunning houses', one with ornate columns, arches and a rose window. A brick-built former chapel in a Devon village has two and a half acres (with triple stable block and large paddock). A Victorian Congregational chapel in Fowey is now three houses – 'many original features including arched leaded windows and exposed old church timbers'. A Grade II listed chapel in Gloucestershire has a galleried sitting area and bedroom with *en suite* shower room. All sound quite enticing, from a house-hunter's point of view. But they come loaded with significance, rich with resonance. The air must be thick with organ and with hymn, with voices united in praise or murmuring in prayer. Emotion, too: the joining in holy matrimony and departing in peace. And who would be able to fix the evening drinks without sensing the outraged glare of the minister?

The Church of England itself appears to take a pragmatic view of this sustained erosion of the ubiquitous visual reminders of what it once was. It can hardly do otherwise, I suppose. Given the unstoppable decline in church attendance over the twentieth century, there is nothing for it but to accept the situation and try to work out the most sensible way to dispose of the plant, as it were. Many people – including my agnostic self – would prefer to see a church doing what it was built to do, but if that is no longer happening then action has to be taken. The Church Commissioners are not keen on conspicuous dereliction or, indeed, on the bulldozers. Both, after all, send out rather unfavourable signals. Admittedly, the site of a demolished church can be sold and the proceeds devoted to some other realm of activity, but the explosion of bricks and dust will still have made a point. As do broken windows and boarded-up doors. Better to diversify and re-invent (bowling alley? wine bar?). And, when needs must, consign to the hands of the heritage industry.

The Church's problem is that it remains inextricably entwined with a widespread surviving physical presence that is no longer an appropriate reflection. A church looks like a church and nothing else, and tends to continue to do so however crafty the conversion. Bowling alley and wine bar may be commercially attractive but do nothing for the image of the Church of England. In this country, cities are peppered with churches and in rural areas you are seldom out of sight of a tower or a steeple. John Ogilby's seventeenth-century road maps used steeple, hill and water as universal navigation signs. You orientated yourself by the visible church, the rising contour, the stream and bridge. Then, that steeple symbol also reflected the universal power and presence of the Church spiritual. Now that it no longer does, this potent burden of stone and brick is both an embarrassment and a liability. But the Church cannot abdicate all responsibility and hand the problem over to the State, even if the relevant government department were prepared to take it on. The Church of England today is eternally linked to all its previous incarnations by the solidity of architecture: the remote chapel, the parish church, the high Victorian gothic extravaganza, the abbeys and cathedrals. And of course the heritage aspect is not always in accord with the pastoral aspect. The Church wants wor-shippers; it frequently has to make do with tourists.

The Church Commissioners do not seek to accelerate the process of church redundancy, except when it has been brought about by pastoral reorganization. They await an approach from the parochial church council, the reluctant admission that it can no longer carry on and keep the church going. Then they step in; the mechanism is set in motion.

The irony here is that the Church of England's own financial levy, the quota, can be the last straw for a struggling church. This is exacted by the Church Commissioners according to a Byzantine system which varies from diocese to diocese. It descends from the various other methods the Church has seized on for financing its clergy and the services thus provided to congregations: glebe land, which could be farmed to provide an income; tithes – the tenth of the income from land, stock or industry due to the incumbent; and, in the nineteenth century, the revenues distributed by the Ecclesiastical Commissioners. The Church Commissioners of today are strapped, apparently. They can no longer meet the whole cost of the clergy's pensions and can only contribute towards the cost of the clergy's pay and housing. The quota fills the gap, church by church, parish by parish. Rodhuish has to find over £1,600 a year and it is a hefty burden. For the diocese of Bath and Wells the assessment is calculated annually on a congregational count. Someone must count heads every Sunday, keep a record, and report back. Then comes the bill – in Rodhuish's case, the quid pro quo is the presence of the rector once a month. On other Sundays, a lay reader officiates.

As one might expect, controversy rages over the quota and who pays how much. Poor parishes and small churches squirm. And should payment be seen as a free-will offering or the response to a perfectly reasonable account for services rendered? Clergy worried by some of the implications of what one might describe as quota rage warn of the dangers of congregationalism.

They are thinking, I take it, of congregationalism with a small 'c' rather than a systematic defection to the embrace of the Congregational Church. But the point is interesting, provocative and makes me realize that my aunt Rachel, loyally C of E all her life, had become in old age a closet congregationalist, infuriated by what she saw as the bureaucracy and detachment of the Church Commissioners. As soon as the lay reader system came into force for Rodhuish she was a convert: 'What do we need a priest for anyway? I much prefer a DIY service.'

It is an ancient enthusiasm. The Congregational Church of today finds its ancestry in the early Christian churches, the small self-supporting sects in which organized religion all began. All that a believer needs is direct access to God within a community of fellow spirits, without the mediation of a priesthood or control by any civil or ecclesiastical power. Before the Reformation, the Anabaptists had seized on this notion of religious liberty. After the Elizabethan Settlement the separatist movement began to gather steam and the Spanish ambassador – presumably rigid with disapproval – reported on one such London group,

a newly invented sect, called by those who belong to it 'the pure or stainless religion'. They meet to the number of 150 in a house where their preacher used a half-tub for a pulpit, and was girded with a white cloth. Each one brought with them whatever food he had at home to eat, and the leaders divided money among those who were poorest, saying that they imitated the life of the Apostles and refused to enter the Temples to partake of the Lord's supper as it was a papistical ceremony.

In the seventeenth century the Independents, as they were known, tended to get subsumed into the whole Puritan movement. The Leyden group of separatists from which the Pilgrim

Fathers sprang included Congregationalists from East Anglia; the *Mayflower* and the Pilgrim Fathers would beget American Puritanism and American Congregationalism with it. But there is, and always has been, a fine distinction between Puritanism and Congregationalism. For the Puritans the church was a national institution. Congregationalism sought independence for individual churches. In its institutional form it is doing as well today as any of the Nonconformist churches. But it is its spirit that has Church of England clergy uneasy, it seems, within the climate of quota confusion and resentment. They may indeed do well to watch their backs. In the last resort, for most worshippers loyalty and commitment is to their local church, just as it always has been, and never mind the bishops and their palaces. Or the Church Commissioners and their committees.

My grandmother and aunt, both devout Christians, were also church tourists. They introduced me to church tourism when I was too ignorant and too young to appreciate what was happening. On any drive or 'trip' close attention was paid to churches. As soon as a spire or tower was spotted, we homed in on it. Assessment began as they went through the lych-gate: good Romanesque doorway, pity about the nineteenth-century windows, those corbels are interesting. Inside, comment and criticism intensified: fascinating misericords, the screen must be very early, lovely hammerbeam roof, hideous kneelers (my grandmother). I trailed behind, staring vacantly, wondering how soon we would be allowed to leave and then maybe stop off somewhere for a cream tea. If the tour was unendurably prolonged, I would sneak out and sit in the porch, glumly reading the Sunday school announcements and the flower-arranging rota (empathizing with whoever it was around here who got landed with the potted-meat jars).

Years later, I caught the bug myself. By then I was living in Oxfordshire with husband and children and I had bought all extant volumes of Pevsner's *Buildings of England* with my first book advance. I 'Pevsnered' every Oxfordshire church (a verb which has not yet achieved the dictionaries, but should). On any car journey, the relevant volumes of Pevsner were stacked up on the back seat. We did the recommended perambulation of market towns and saved till last the church – the treat and centrepiece – tacitly respecting the significance of religion as both a historical and architectural phenomenon. We entered churches as unbelievers, but acutely conscious of every resonance. All that beauty, all that faith. So much intransigence, oppression, exploitation, intolerance. So much suffering, heroism, endurance. And every bit of it somehow represented and recorded by brick, stone and glass.

Landscape mutates. It must. The landscape of this country bears the imprint of much that has happened, not least the landscape of cities, towns and villages. Religion and religious change have been central to our history; churches are the most eloquent of all those physical testimonies. I remember that once during those church visits of my adolescence I emerged from boredom and incuriosity to ask about the headless effigies over a doorway. And thus learned about iconoclasm and had a sudden startling insight into the power of prejudice and conviction and coercion. That such things could finger – could have fingered – that slumbering Devon village. And I remember too a moment of aesthetic perception – looking up at the fan-vaulting of a cathedral and realizing that it mirrored the canopy of a beech wood and must have been thus inspired. For a while the lust for a cream tea receded, and the place came alive.

The established churches of this country are today marginalized institutions. Since about 1700 we have been both a secular and a tolerant society by comparison with most other European countries. But the slide towards secularization has been most precipitate in the twentieth century. Patterns of church attendance vary of course between country and city; industrialization meant a steady erosion of the traditional Sunday church-going habit. In 1851 around 40 per cent of the population would have attended at least one church service a week. It was the heyday of the village church as community centre and social indicator, as described by Owen Chadwick, the historian of the Victorian Church:

The squire was in his pew, his friend the parson in his stall, respectable farmers in pews, and on the benches the labourers in smock frocks, delicately embroidered at front and back, their wives often in scarlet flannel shawls. The men sat passive, not following in books, some unable to read, but silent with a solid attentiveness, not liking to be absent because of the squire or the farmer or habit, but in no way sorry to be there, men without hostility and with quiet acceptance.

The 'quiet acceptance', if such it was, must surely have been a surface feature, if you think of agricultural unrest both earlier and to come, but the general picture is clear, and very similar to that conjured up by Richard Gough, writing of his community of 150 years earlier. The Victorian Church underwrote society itself.

By the early twentieth century church-going was already a minority custom. Overall attendance had fallen to around 25 per cent, with 20 per cent in cities and 30 in the country. The village church was evidently clinging on with a little more success. But religion was still a central feature in Edwardian society. Two thirds of all infants were baptized. Church parade was compulsory in the army as college chapel was at university. It was as the century progressed that defection accelerated. By 1950 the national rate of church attendance had dipped to 10 per cent (the end-of-century figure was 8 per cent, and falling). That was the point at which I was sitting in the customary pew at Rodhuish, with a dozen or so other people. Since the total population of the hamlet was then around seventy, St Bartholomew's was not doing too badly.

Why have most people ceased to go to church? Clearly there can be no simple answer, but perhaps first of all one needs to ask why any go in the first place. Are they in search of spiritual solace or does membership of a church fulfil some other need? For many people both may be true – certainly that was the case with my grandmother. And of course a church in order to flourish needs both factors to apply. People must feel that religious belief is a comfort and a support and they must also need the reassurance of a like-minded community. This last is the sociological and anthropological explanation for religious adherence, through space and time: in the words of Emile Durkheim, 'Rites are the means whereby a social group reaffirms itself.'

The Roman Catholic Church has been more successful in retaining membership than the Church of England or the Nonconformist churches, for obvious reasons. The looser and less insistent connection between the Protestant churches and their adherents was always bound to make them more vulnerable to the tide of secularization. It is when the age level of church attenders rises that the institution is in danger. When church-going is a family activity and the commitment of children is fostered by that of their parents, the priest doesn't have to worry too much. And the Roman Catholic Church sees to it that this happens. Interestingly, the demise of Sunday schools seems to have played a significant part in the falling-off of faith, or at least of church attendance, among the Protestant churches. Back in the early part of the twentieth century, they still retained some of their Victorian prestige as valued sources of educational opportunity. But they also provided free child care for harassed and overworked mothers – no wonder they were popular and no wonder the church recognized that they were expedient.

When visiting a church these days I look out for evidence of a Sunday school, and it is often there, in the form of a lavish display of pinned-up artwork. There has been much finger-painting of baby Jesuses and camels and palm trees. Sometimes there is a nook beside the vestry with a low table and small chairs. And I remember that my own first-ever experience of a school situation was a Sunday school. It took place in the grounds of the Bishop's Palace in Khartoum, in steamy Sudanese heat. I was about nine and had never been to school, so I shared the awed sense of privilege of the Victorian child. I thought it was wonderful. The exercise book and sharpened pencils. The other children, also done up in Sunday best: clean cotton frocks, white socks and hair-ribbons for the girls, shorts for the boys, with shirt and tie. We read a chapter from Genesis and then answered questions. My hand shot up: I was a child well versed in the Authorized Version, tales of Greece and Rome, *The Arabian Nights* and not much else. We copied out a psalm in best handwriting. We drew a picture of the Holy Family on the flight into Egypt (no difficulty with palm trees and camels – most of us had grown up knowing nothing else). I got red ticks and a gold star and went home a devout member of the Church of England. I'd have been theirs for life, if they'd cared to follow through.

For a church to thrive, recruitment is crucial. Ideally, that recruitment which stems from established family practice. Generation follows generation and the congregation remains well stocked of a Sunday. And for this to happen it seems that there has to be this fusion of spiritual and social needs. In the twentieth century, both have been seriously eroded. Many people still believe in a God, but the requirements of believers have changed. Belief has become something more personal, a private commitment rather than a public affirmation. In 1938 a Church of England Commission could talk of 'a living God, on whose act of will creation itself depends, and who has a purpose for mankind, to accomplish which He is Himself active in history'. In the wake of the First World War, this seems a rash statement. The theodicy question and David Hume rise up in indignation: 'Is he willing to prevent evil but not able? Then is he impotent. Is he able but not willing? Then is he malevolent. Is he both able and willing? Whence then is evil?' After 1945, those claims were wisely dropped. The Church of England's interpretation of the nature of God today would seem to be rather different. But while that 1938 declaration may have looked a touch archaic even then, it is of course entirely accurate in terms of the traditional understanding of the divine role. God directs and intervenes. Things happen by His grace; He disposes. He thus ordains society, and not just private fates.

But when the social order changes dramatically, as it has over the course of the last century, people's perception of society changes, as do their communal requirements. Organized religion flourishes in social groups such as the enclosed unit of the village, or work-centred communities based around mining, fishing and agriculture, for example. Nineteenth-century changes in patterns of employment and the advent of cheaper transport did much to erode the self-contained community. Industrialization opened the way to wider influences and other ways of bonding. The pub, the football pitch, the Sunday outing. When the Sunday church service is no longer the only time and place at which you can be sure of meeting up with friends, neighbours and relatives, then a subtle aspect of its allure is threatened. 'I'll be able to have a word with Mrs So-and-So on Sunday,' my grandmother would say. After the service, there was much standing around and chatting outside the church. There still is at St Bartholomew's, and long may it continue.

Any church is also a museum and an art gallery. One of the most consistently rewarding moments when Pevsnering a church is turning to the furnishings section after the main perambulation. There you are confronted with the tangible evidence of individual commitment over the centuries, the memorial plaques and the brasses and the tombs and the effigies. Those who wanted to make sure that we would take note of their names – and their status and their piety. And there also is the display of creativity. The gifts lavished upon the church in the name of God – and the salvation of the donors' souls. The carved screens and the paintings and the lecterns and the brass-bound Bibles. The embroideries.

I always take a look at the kneelers, in tribute to my grandmother. The salvation of souls is out of fashion now as a motive for church embellishment. Kneelers usually stem from a local body – the Mothers' Union, the Women's Institute, or a craft organization – and would seem to be prompted by social involvement and, perhaps, a sense of commitment to the church. My grandmother was a superb needlewoman and her inspection of kneelers was that of a connoisseur. They seldom came up to scratch. Sometimes they gave such offence that we had to curtail our visit to that particular church. They invariably fell short in terms of either colour combinations or technical achievement: harsh primary colours, patterns taken from a book, nothing more ambitious than a basic cross-stitch or, at most, a stab at the Berlin woolwork so beloved of the nineteenth century.

The chapel at Rodhuish is of basic simplicity within – whitewashed walls, tiled floor, simple carved pews. Modest pulpit – not that of the potted-meat jar ordeals, which I remember as a large, ornate and forbidding structure. There are wrought-iron candlesticks at the ends of the pews, and a brass pair on the altar; and a fine candelabra by Jim Horrabin, a distinguished artist-blacksmith who lives locally. Nearly all the rest of the furnishings were created by my aunt and grandmother, over the years. Rachel's metalwork sculpture of Jacob wrestling with the angel stands near to the altar. Her carved altar screen with trumpeting angels at either end holds up a linen altar curtain topped by a border of my grandmother's superb green and blue wool tapestry. More of her work frames the altar itself. There are two large kneelers, one at either side of the altar. And from the lectern hangs a banner in Assisi work – a flight of blue and white swallows.

Looking today at this work – at my grandmother's chair-seats, her sampler, the evening bag she made for me when I was seventeen, at the piles of Assisi-work mats and tray cloths and table runners that I would never dare to use – I recognize a remarkable talent. Indeed, pursuing the whole matter – conjuring up information on textiles and embroidery in the British Library to find out what she was doing – I realize that she was in the top league, in the first flight. She was a mistress of the art, or craft, or whatever it is. I pore over illustrations of embroidery from museums and galleries and see that her work is just as good, indeed much of it is better. And all through my adolescence I sat at the other end of the sofa of an evening, while she planned and pondered and stitched, and I paid little or no attention. At one point, she put needle and canvas into my hands and tried to get me going. Hopeless. No powers of application, no talent.

Now I understand her brisk dismissal of run-of-the-mill church embroidery. She was the professional casting an eye at an exhibition of Sunday painters. She knew quite well that what she was doing was of another order. Indeed, she exhibited her work occasionally. But would never have sold it, which makes the term professional inappropriate, I suppose. She did it in the long tradition of women making beautiful things at home for their own consumption or that of their friends, and to adorn the local church.

She did Assisi work and what seems usually to be called Winchester work. The Assisi work came first. This is a special form of cross-stitch on linen, using a method known as voiding, in which it is the background that is embroidered rather than the design, which then stands out in white or cream linen against the darker stitching, traditionally red, though blue and green are also used. The principal motifs are nearly always symmetrically arranged animal pairs, mostly birds, which are then surrounded with filigree scrollwork in Holbein stitch, a double running stitch used also to outline the motifs. A large Assisi-work piece of my grandmother's has a border of dove pairs tumbling around the central square, a crisp and elegant harmony of blue and cream. In another, the outlined creatures look like stylized dolphins. Both the designs and technique of Assisi work are based on an ancient Italian tradition reaching back into the Middle Ages, but which had fallen into disuse until revived in the early 1900s in an Assisi convent as a means for poor women to supplement the family income. Tablecloths and napkins were turned out instead of the time-honoured altar cloths and chasubles, and a nice little line established for the tourist trade. Maybe that is where my grandmother first saw the work, on one of the Grand Tours of her girlhood. The voiding idea, incidentally, seems to have perhaps come from the technique of woodcuts, way back, while Holbein stitch gets its name from Hans Holbein the Younger, many of whose paintings show clothes embroidered with double running stitch. And the favoured bird motifs surely have resonances of St Francis.

Assisi work is a highly formalized craft. Most of the patterns would have come out of books, but the tried practitioner plays around with these. My grandmother's patterns are not quite like other people's. Her doves are somehow plumper and more skittish, her dolphins distinctly idiosyncratic. And the blue and white banner of swallows at Rodhuish is entirely her own design, I suspect, while remaining true to the basic principles of the craft.

At some point in the 1930s my grandmother discovered Winchester work. This now became her favoured medium, and the ensuing twenty years or so were her most richly productive, when she was in her fifties and sixties. Winchester work is named for the finest flowerings of the style, which are the 360 kneelers, along with alms bags, cushions and other furnishings created by the Winchester Broderers and presented to the city's cathedral in 1936. But thereby hangs a tale, of which the heroine is a splendid lady called Miss Louisa Pesel. Miss Pesel was a Yorkshirewoman born in Bradford in 1870 who settled in Hampshire in mid-life. She was by then a renowned craftswoman who had been presented with a gold chatelaine (a decorative pendant worn on the lapel, apparently) by the Worshipful Company of Broderers in 1914 in recognition of her work for the study and revival of embroidery in England. But she had also spent five years in Athens as designer to the Royal Hellenic School of Needlework and Lace. A set of specially commissioned samplers by her is in the Victoria and Albert Museum. She was the author of a string of publications such as *Practical Canvas Embroidery*, *Stitches from Eastern Embroideries*, and so forth. One of these titles has a pompous introduction by the then Slade Professor of Fine Art at Oxford, which I would have slung right back at him had I been Miss Louisa Pesel:

One of the ways in which civilized man [*sic*], the victim of boredom, machinery, mass-production and standardized culture, tries to recapture something of the zest of a primitive life of personal achievement is the making with his [*sic*, again] own hands of beautiful things. The skill required for such work is often slight; and dexterity has not yet ceased to be the birthright of the race. But the ability to make a thing which is not only a 'good job' but also beautiful is a rare gift, and much first-rate craftsmanship goes to the making of objects which, from poverty or imperfection of design, fail to achieve beauty. Of no craft is this more true than Embroidery . . . Miss Pesel's admirable handbooks on various traditional stitches come to the assistance of the worker exactly where, in the matter of formal design, he (or she) is weakest . . .

To be fair, I suppose he is having to go at precisely the sort of mundane work that so offended my grandmother, and at least he eventually concedes the existence of women, but the tone is insufferably patronizing. I suppose Miss Pesel needed the endorsement of academia, but in fact her own handbooks are most scholarly in their attributions and explanations, while being briskly instructive.

And now I see the source of my grandmother's inspiration. I look at illustrations of work done under Miss Pesel's aegis and the familiar identifying qualities of my grandmother's creations spring out at me. There are the robust central cross motifs, the scrolled borders. There are the neat squares with a central eye, the smooth double lines. And there above all are the shaded backgrounds and the subtle palette.

Colour is crucial in Winchester work. My grandmother's palette was principally blues, often with a buff background. But the blues run across a whole spectrum so that the effect is soft and melting, while the background too is worked in different shades, giving it depth and interest. She also used a rich plum fading into pink, sometimes combined with the blues. The wools were expertly dyed and came from some specialist supplier – I do remember the sensuous quality of those little hanks of pure colour lined up in her workbox, a swathe of cherry, rose and salmon, a peacock range from indigo to sky blue. The base was coarse linen hessian and always to hand was the sheet of squared paper to which my grandmother constantly referred – the architect's design on which she had worked for weeks before ever picking up the needle. Winchester work is counted thread work, in which each stitch is pre-ordained. It derives from the English tradition of cross-stitch design as used in samplers. Miss Pesel was an authority on seventeenth-century samplers and her initial venture into the style that was to blossom into the full glory of Winchester work took their angular motifs and turned them into abstract designs. This first flowering produced the cushions and kneelers for the Bishop of Winchester's private chapel in Wolvesey Palace, for which she formed and supervised the Wolvesey Canvas Embroidery Guild.

She ran a tight ship, I would imagine. No messing. No flights of individual fancy, and limited tea-breaks only. I warm to Miss Pesel. She seems a Gertrude Jekyll-like figure, one of those steely, industrious, inspired early twentieth-century women who beaver away and revolutionize an entire activity. Gertrude Jekyll affected the gardening habits of two generations. For the initiated, Miss Pesel's enlightened skill meant that church kneelers could never be quite the same again.

From the Golsoncott gong stand to Miss Louisa Pesel, by way of tree-worship and a good deal else. But the central matter of this chapter is the ambivalent position of the established churches, as the new century gets under way. They are hanging on by a toenail, as institutions, but we are reminded of them wherever we look. It is hard to be out of sight of a church or chapel, whatever it may be doing today to earn its keep. When my grandchildren were small I used to entertain them with that hand game: 'Here's the church and here's the steeple, Open the doors and there's the people . . .' But the people are not there, and like as not the doors will be bolted against larceny. There must be plenty of children in the country today who have seldom or never set foot inside a church. In 1999 Dr George Carey, the Archbishop of Canterbury, spoke of Britain having an 'allergy to religion'. He was addressing an audience of clergy assembled to analyse the Church of England's Decade of Evangelism, a campaign which had apparently been tough going. 'We are a society oppressed not by lack but by surfeit, not by strife but by ease,' he told them, calling for a fresh approach to the mission which would engage with contemporary culture. He was correct enough in identifying the problem as one of social disengagement. And perhaps accurate also in implying – whether deliberately or not – that piety thrives on deprivation and discord.

St Bartholomew's, Rodhuish, may not make it far into the twenty-first century as an operative place of worship. The Churches Conservation Trust will acquire further clients, and the estate agents a satisfactory supply of beguiling conversions. But the physical reminders of what once was are inextinguishable. It is all still out there in the landscape: faith, hope, charity – bigotry, oppression, persecution.

The Woman in White and the Boy on the Beach

When I was mooching about the Somerset lanes as an adolescent, waiting for life to begin, I saw Golsoncott as a place where nothing ever happened. I thought of it fondly, but reckoned that it was elsewhere that things went on and that in due course one would go forth to elsewhere, with all that that implied. And so I did, but in due course also Golsoncott became a retreat, a haven when rather too much was happening, the stable element in an unreliable world, a kind of Jamesian great good place. You could know that it would always be the same, year by year. Absence of event was now the treasured aspect.

During the seventy years of the family's occupation of the house no one was born there. Three people died: my grandfather in 1941, my grandmother thirty-four years later, and finally my aunt Rachel. Events of a significant kind. To a fifteen-year-old, things happening means a bit of *Sturm und Drang* in daily life, and Golsoncott was indeed fairly immune to that. One calm rural day slid blandly into the next, with only the weather serving up any potent kind of change. And even that interference with prescribed routine was sternly resisted: family ethos was that you ignored weather and simply did what you had intended to do. You went for a walk in the rain; that was what raincoats were for.

Looking back, it seems that the sunlight through the wisteria spattered the veranda tiles in exactly the same way in 1995 as it did on my arrival from Egypt in 1945, a footstep on the boot-scraper sounded exactly the same over five decades, the latch of the kitchen-garden gate struck the same note. The place stood still; people came and went and grew and changed, elsewhere all was sound and fury. True, but a profoundly deceptive truth. In fact, what the place was doing was secretly recording, bearing witness to the events that apparently passed it by, turning itself into a signifier for the century. All the things that did not happen here were nevertheless being taken down and held in evidence. One day, the place would speak with tongues.

In 1941 my grandmother was at work on her sampler of Golsoncott. Elsewhere, other things were going on. The row of stylized embroidered evacuees posed at the bottom of her canvas; in London, the bombs were falling on their homes. In June, Hitler's armies invaded Russia. On the far side of the world, in December, the Japanese attacked the United States fleet at Pearl Harbor, Hong Kong fell. Throughout 1941, in the deserts of north Africa, the Libyan campaign was in full flow. The following year, Rommel's tanks would be rolling east-wards; my mother and I would become a part of the British exodus to Palestine in anticipation of the possible – probable, indeed – fall of Egypt. My grandmother must have thought much about us, but already I hardly remembered her. My aunt Rachel was in London, sorting out evacuee families from Stepney, sketching the blasted landscape of London in snatched moments – work notes for future paintings – and dashing down to Golsoncott for a few days when she could. My grandmother must have embroidered and gardened, just as she always had, but with a sense of the world smoking beyond her horizon.

Golsoncott rode out the war and the whole century. An easy ride, one may think. But the shadows are around – the

84

long shadows of what happened in other places. One of these is there on an August afternoon of 1933, brushing across the swing seat with the awning, on the Golsoncott veranda. Another old photograph: my grandmother sits in the middle of the seat, with a fair-haired teenager on one side of her and my young mother on the other. I am present – a five-month-old baby on my mother's lap. Behind the seat, leaning over, is a sharp-featured boy of around thirteen. A dark girl, slightly younger, sits at my grandmother's feet. My grandmother and my mother are gazing at me – statutory baby-worship for the photo opportunity. The other three children look politely bored.

There is someone else seated in a basket chair, slightly apart from the group on the swing seat. A woman in a white dress – neat pointed face, dark hair with a centre parting. She is turned away from the rest of us, detached, pensive, one hand resting behind her head, her legs elegantly furled.

This is Mary Britnieva, born in St Petersburg in 1890. Two of the children – her two – were born in Russia during the Red Terror. Her husband was killed by the Bolsheviks.

When Mary met my grandmother she was a widow in her early forties, extremely hard up, struggling to provide her children, Tsapik and Maria, with the kind of upbringing and education they might have expected had history not picked off their father and wiped out the family wealth. Her father was British, a St Petersburg diamond merchant called Charles Bucknall, himself born in Russia, who amassed a considerable fortune during his thirty years of trading in the Russian city. He was a member of the significant British merchant and industrial communities in Russia during the late nineteenth and early twentieth centuries. Unusually, he married a Russian girl – Antonina Pavlovna Mikoulova-Ananevskaya.

The expatriate community on the whole kept a stern hold on their British identity, so such a liaison was something of a departure and, equally, may well have been looked upon with some misgivings by Antonina's aristocratic landowning family.

That pre-Revolutionary British community in Russia can be conjured up still from the pages of the 1914 edition of Baedeker. St Petersburg: pop. 2,075,000 – which includes 2,100 Englishmen, 11,200 Germans and 2,400 Frenchmen. Women entirely omitted, one notes, or, more probably, subsumed into that total. And the support system of this British (a more appropriate term, since there was a large Scottish element) expatriate society is meticulously entered. The Clubs: New English Club (for Englishmen and Americans), the Imperial Yacht Club (for the high aristocracy and diplomatic corps), the English Club (for the nobility and high officials). The four English-speaking doctors. The English booksellers: Watkins. And P. Botkin & Sons, Nevski 38, suppliers of tea.

The St Petersburg British community was larger than that in Moscow and stemmed from the end of the eighteenth century, by which time it already numbered around 1,500 – shipbuilders, naval and military personnel, engineers and doctors, craftsmen. As the administrative and diplomatic centre of the Russian Empire, St Petersburg condescended to Moscow, being perceived as sophisticated and cosmopolitan where Moscow was commercial, industrial and deeply Russian. But it was in Moscow that the Smiths held sway, a family of enterprising Scottish boiler-makers – their story told by Harvey Pitcher in his book *The Smiths of Moscow, A Story of Britons Abroad*, the climate of that time also marvellously evoked by Penelope Fitzgerald in her novel *The Beginning of Spring*. The Smith factory flourished for a couple of generations, valiantly adapting to economic circumstances and the exigencies of the political climate. The Smiths have left an abiding legacy: they introduced their Russian workers to football (partly in a bid to divert their attention from vodka) – today it is Russia's most popular sport.

It is fascinating to contemplate with the wisdom of hindsight the trajectories of utterly disparate lives that will one day intersect. In the years before 1914 my grandmother was bringing up her young family in St Albans, secure in Edwardian England. Fifteen hundred miles away, Mary Britnieva was a girl in St Petersburg. Back then, this unlikely conjunction of lives and persons would indeed have seemed improbable. For my grandmother, Russia must have seemed a place a long way away that was nothing much to do with her. Mary Britnieva, although half English, had grown up in Russia, spoke French within the family and Russian to everyone else and presumably saw her future as firmly located in St Petersburg. But barely twenty years later, there they are together in west Somerset on an August afternoon. History had stepped in, exerting its inexorable control. Mary Britnieva had drawn the short straw.

One of the worst plights of the twentieth century has been to be Russian – at any point. They fought in the Great War with the other Allies. Then came the Revolution. Then the Civil War. Then the Red Terror. Then the Second World War. And beyond all this there was Stalin: Siberia lay in wait, and the gulags. Those of us who have spent most of our life in a politically stable country in peacetime can only look back in horror. And in ignorance. This is a dimension of distress that is barely conceivable.

In 1984 I went to the Soviet Union, as it then was, as a member of a delegation of six British writers sent by the Great Britain–USSR Association to have talks with representatives of the Soviet Writers' Union. Before *perestroika*, before *glasnost*. We spent six days in Moscow, sitting round an immense table, hemmed in by all the paraphernalia of international exchange – simultaneous translators, TV cameras, overwrought organizers rushing hither and thither. By day, we discussed such matters as traditional forms of narrative, the role of the short story, fictions of provincial life and so forth, sternly resisting provocative attempts to draw us into a political dialogue. The visiting team addressed the subjects on the agenda, each speaking for the five minutes allocated by earlier agreement; our hosts talked about anything that came into their heads, at entirely unpredictable length. I understood for the first time why delegates at international conferences emerge looking dazed and haggard; it is simply that they have been exposed to the Russian style of debate.

In the evenings, we were wined and dined. Interminable meals punctuated by toasts: they toasted us, we toasted them, desperately scraping the barrel for further toast proposals – peace and friendship, literature, language, Pushkin, Tolstoy, Shakespeare, the chef responsible for this excellent dinner . . . Usually these occasions took place in hotels or the sumptuous headquarters of the Soviet Writers' Union (next door to the original of the Rostov mansion in *War and Peace*) but on a more relaxed occasion we were invited to the home of one participant Soviet writer. A small apartment in a shabby block – bedroom, sitting-room, bathroom and a passage that incorporated the cooking facilities. This was relative luxury – he was a favoured figure and accordingly privileged. We all squeezed in somehow. We ate, we drank, we toasted. And we Brits felt humbled, looking around furtively at the ugly, utilitarian furnishings, at all the evidence of making do, getting by. But what I remember best is the coffee cup. A pretty flowered bone-china cup – nineteenth-century, by the look of it. Just one, amid a hotchpotch of cracked and mismatched crockery. Our hostess was sitting next to me – I admired the cup. She told me that it had belonged to her mother: 'It is all that she had left from her home, after the war. Just that. Nothing else.'

One coffee cup. I thought of households elsewhere, the world over, crammed with the bits and pieces that sift down from generation to generation. The chairs and tables and rugs and pictures and knick-knacks that conjure up other times and other places and people no longer alive.

One coffee cup.

Mary Britnieva came into my grandmother's life because she was staying one summer with her sister Agnes who had rented a house in nearby Washford. My grandmother, hearing of this interesting alien ménage, invited the children up to Golsoncott for tea. Maria managed to fall into the rose-garden pond (most visiting children did, sooner or later), was dried off in the bathroom and returned to her mother with ecstatic stories of the green bath and the lavish garden. They visited again, and again. Their mother came too. And so it all began – an association between the two families that would continue unto the third generation.

My grandmother and Rachel seem initially to have been mesmerized by the Britneffs – principally by their exuberance and volatility. They became frequent long-term visitors at Golsoncott, Mary's Russian mother by then included. 'One used to hear them having splendid rows and throwing plates at each other,' Rachel would say appreciatively, years later, making a comparison I suppose with her own more sober home life. Golsoncott plates? Or is this a memory of the *émigré* enclave in London in which they lived and where she certainly visited them?

My grandparents took over financial responsibility for Tsapik's education. Britneff family history has it that they also funded the unsuccessful action which Mary's father brought against the King in the High Court of Justice in 1930 for the recovery of cash and jewellery deposited by him with the British Embassy in Petrograd in 1918, for safekeeping by the British Government. Some £58,000 in Russian notes, with jewellery and precious stones worth a further £58,000. A considerable fortune. *Bucknall* v. *the King*, before Mr Justice Horridge, in the King's Bench Division. The *Times* report is full of impenetrable jargon about demurrers and bailment and much invoking of the Indemnity Act of 1920, but laced with mentions of a locked leather bag subsequently found open and empty, behind which smokes the reality of that time. What had happened was that 'the Embassy premises were forcibly entered by persons claiming to be representatives of the Soviet Government', during which episode the valuables went missing. Charles Bucknall held the British Government responsible for the loss of his property; the Government denied liability, and won.

During the 1930s Mary Britnieva published two books about her experiences before, during and in the wake of the Revolution – *One Woman's Story* and *A Stranger in Your Midst* – substantial parts of both having been written at Golsoncott. The books were enthusiastically received and for a while she enjoyed a certain celebrity. Her account of the raid on the British Embassy at Petrograd in 1918, of which her brother and sister-in-law were eyewitnesses, attracted particular attention. The naval attaché, Captain Cromie, was shot by the Bolshevik intruders. And elsewhere in the building, someone was hastily helping themselves to the contents of that leather bag.

In 1914 Mary was twenty-four. She signed up as a Red Cross

nurse with the Sisters of Mercy and went at once to the West Prussian front. A baptism of fire. She describes her first patients – a German with his liver shot to pieces, a Caucasian with an amputated leg – and the brisk comment of the head doctor: 'If all the nurses are going to weep like this over every death-case, we shall all be drowned.' Later, she sees a battlefield with frozen Russian bodies with their boots expediently stolen: 'Fieldmice had made a nest in the head of one.' Near Warsaw, the hospital occupied Teresino Palace, the country seat of a Polish prince, where she nursed an endless stream of gangren-ous wounded in panelled rooms hung with tapestries. A gas attack nearby left the 21st Siberian Regiment almost wiped out and the nurses trying to work in a field strewn with men 'lying motionless in orderly rows as far as the eye could reach . . . Their upturned faces terribly swollen and livid . . . their bloodshot eyes protruding, unable to utter a word, yet fully conscious.'

In the midst of this carnage, her own future was determined. In 1916, she became engaged to the briskly spoken head doctor. Alexander Britneff was twenty years her senior, himself the son of an army doctor who had been Physician-in-Ordinary to Dowager Empress Marie Feodorovna (wife of Emperor Alexander III). The Britneffs were married in early 1918. The Tsar had abdicated the previous year (and would be executed in July 1918) and 'these new-fangled persons who called them-selves Bolsheviks' had seized power. It is apparent that Mary was entirely unpolitical. She had been growing up amid the unrest and discontent of the pre-revolutionary period, but the events of 1917 seem to have ambushed her. Now back in Petrograd, the couple were pitched from the horrors of the war to the absolute precariousness of life under Bolshevik rule. Wholesale arrests were common – 'complete trams were being stopped suddenly and all the passengers would be marched off like sheep to the Cheka [secret police] head-quarters, to be sorted, like sheep again, and as inexplicably released a few days later, unless they were detained, in which case they were never heard of again.'

The Bucknall family was still in Petrograd. Their home became a centre for assembling food parcels to be sent to prisoners in the Peter and Paul fortress, where foreigners arrested by the Bolsheviks were incarcerated. One of Mary's brothers was in there, receiving messages and money from his wife, ingeniously smuggled by prising up the metal sardine clamped to the top of Amieux Frères sardine tins. The prisoners were crammed twenty to a cell designed for one and even included the British Consul at one point. Young Bucknall was released after thirteen weeks, but the family now realized that they must leave. The Consul arranged for Charles Bucknall and his youngest daughter to leave with the consular party, with the rest of the family due to follow as soon as they could arrange for the disposal of their possessions.

Except for Mary, who elected to stay with her husband. And so was plunged now into the perils and privations of the Civil War, the famine and the years of the Terror. Alexander Britneff was mobilized by the Red Army and ordered to form the First Red Army Surgical Hospital and take it to the front. The prospect of serving under the Bolsheviks was deeply repugnant to him, but he took the view that it was his duty as a doctor to alleviate suffering, whatever the circumstances.

Mary went with him. For the next year or so they moved around Russia in hospital trains, accommodated sometimes in cattle trucks that were marooned in heavy snows. Mary became pregnant. Extraordinarily, she writes, 'I was feeling wonderfully fit and well and thoroughly enjoyed the strange wandering throughout Russia, in spite of the rough surroundings and conditions.' And it may indeed have been preferable to the preceding months in Petrograd, already hit by famine, with cats and dogs slaughtered to be sold in the markets and 'decently clad men and women with grey, hollowed cheeks and great burning eyes'.

But the respite was not to last. In 1919 the couple were back in Petrograd, where Tsapik was born. When Alexander Britneff returned to the front his wife and baby son remained in the city, where they were to endure the conditions brought about by the Civil War and ensuing chaos. During her travels with the hospital unit Mary had seen the pathetic fall-out from the Great War, the Revolution and the Civil War – the 'waifs', the *bezprizorniye*: 'In droves they moved over the face of Russia, following the sun and the rumours of food.' Now, in her own home town, she herself lived with this stark deprivation in full view.

The Bolshevik control of the food supply was absolute. Rations were divided into three categories, with Red Army soldiers, bureaucrats and vital workers receiving the highest order, other workers the second (which was less than adequate) and *burzhoois* getting the entirely inadequate third category. The fatally bourgeois Britneffs and their like would have got that, described by Zinoviev as 'just enough bread not to forget the smell of it'. For anything else they had to scavenge or negotiate. Mary gives an account of the barter system that sprang up – the *meshetchniki*, bag carriers who would collect clothes and household articles to take to outlying villages which they would trade with the peasants for flour, cereals, meat and eggs. It was not permitted for peasants to bring food to sell within the city: the vacuum was thus created into which stepped this army of entrepreneurs, many of whom could not be trusted. Housewives stripped themselves of their possessions for a scraggy chicken or a bag of flour.

Over 5 million people died of starvation during those fearful years. Those who survived – and those who didn't – ate rats, mice, grass and weeds. They made flour from acorns, sawdust, clay and horse manure. In some appalling circumstances they ate each other; cannibalism was a grim fact of the famine.

By 1922 it had become clear to both Mary Britnieva and her husband that she must leave Russia. She now had a second child, Maria. Both children were severely undernourished and developing rickets. Mary negotiated for permission to leave; after five months' delay she was examined by a committee of doctors presided over by a commissar and pronounced 80 per cent invalid – sufficient disability, it seems, to warrant application for a passport. When at last Mary arrived in England and was reunited with her parents, the thirteen-month-old Maria weighed only twelve pounds.

For the next few years Alexander Britneff maintained precarious communications with his wife. She had been allowed out only because of her dual nationality. He himself was quite unable to escape. And he was a suspect figure, because of having been doctor to the British Consul in Leningrad (as the city became in 1924). The Bolsheviks were paranoiac about foreign spies, convinced that the regime was encircled by enemies against whom there must be constant vigilance, both internal and external. Just as Britneff had managed to secure himself a job as ship's doctor on a steamer plying the Baltic and calling in at London (where Mary was), he was arrested. He failed to arrive as expected. Mary learned what had happened, and promptly boarded the ship herself to go back to Leningrad and plead his case. She was told he was a British spy and would probably go to Siberia. She seems to have been preparing to follow him there when he was suddenly released, in one of those inexplicable moves so typical of the regime.

The game of cat and mouse continued for Alexander Britneff for another six years. During that time Mary returned to England – torn between husband and children – and then came back once more to the Soviet Union. While she was there her husband wangled the job of ship's doctor again, as a way to make trips to London to visit the children, being cared for by their grandparents. His wife's presence in the Soviet Union would ensure that he did not jump ship. Eventually she could not bear the separation from the children and went back to London where, in 1930, Mary heard that Alexander had been arrested once more.

Back she went to Leningrad, to lay siege to the OGPU offices (successor to the Cheka), begging for information. For two months she was turned away each time she presented herself, then told that she would have to go to Moscow to find out what her husband's sentence might be. Weeks more of stalling and excuses in Moscow, only for an official to announce at last that the file had never left Leningrad. The official added an ominous coda: 'Citizen, though I have told you to hurry back, you had better not be too hopeful. You may be too late. Perhaps several months too late.'

Alexander Britneff had been killed by the Bolsheviks soon after his wife arrived in Leningrad on her determined quest. A spy in the pay of the British Government – that was the charge. Many years later the Foreign Office obtained his death certificate for her from the secret archives of the Leningrad OGPU.

Mary Britnieva's two books are anecdotal, emotional, vivid and sometimes confusing. The second repeats with minor differences some of the principal events of the earlier book.

She relates entire conversations, with apparent total recall, as though the hurtling events of that time had compacted within her mind into a continuous echoing present. In that sense they are a potent reflection of an extraordinary experience. I think of her sitting in the eventless tranquillity of Golsoncott, getting it all down, carrying in her head another world. One embarrassing product of her success as an author, after the translation into German of *One Woman's Story*, was the award of a literary prize by the Führer in 1938. It seems unlikely that Hitler actually read the book, but the German title (*The Sun Sank in the East*) and its indictment of the Soviet regime would have appealed to his advisers. Mary went to Berlin to receive the award from the Führer himself, in what now seems a rather unconsidered move.

Poor little rickety Maria blossomed nicely in England as a child ballerina and did a short stint with the visiting Ballet Russe de Monte Carlo under the direction of Massine. In later life she became an actress, married a lord and, in a further bizarre intersection of trajectories, formed an intense friendship with Tennessee Williams, managing his literary estate after his death and ferociously defending his interests and reputation.

Tsapik served with the British Army during the Second World War and fought at Arnhem. The third child in the photograph, Sandra, Mary Britnieva's niece, died in youth. Tsapik's son Anthony Britneff, my aunt Rachel's godson, was a frequent visitor to Golsoncott. He now lives in British Columbia and has provided further material on his family's traumatic history.

In 1941 my grandmother still rented a beach hut at Blue Anchor, near Watchet. That strip of coast had always been –

and still is – a favoured place for family outings: the Blue Lias cliffs with their seams of pink and grey alabaster, the pebbled shore with its treasure trove of fossils, the melting grey-brown distances of the Bristol Channel. A photograph taken in that year shows a boy standing on the shingle. He wears grey flannel trousers and tweed jacket; he is smiling. This is Otto Kun, born in Vienna in 1924.

Otto came to England at the end of June 1939, at the age of fifteen. His parents had died when he was younger and he was cared for by his grandmother. After *Kristallnacht* (when he was rounded up by the storm troopers but later released) she made strenuous efforts to get the boy out of the country, finally securing an Agricultural Trainee Permit for entry to England. Thus Otto turned up at Toynbee Hall in Stepney, which seems to have served as a clearing station for such arrivals. And thus he came into the ambit of my aunt Rachel, in her capacity as a voluntary helper. She swept him off to Somerset, along with another lad, in 'a dark green Rover 14 saloon with beautiful green leather upholstery'. The precision of Otto's memory can be relied on (and it proved useful in later life). Even amid the trauma of that time he was alert to the details of a car; his interest heralds his eventual flourishing career in industry.

Otto was not a part of the *Kindertransport* – the children's transports – but his experience runs parallel to that of the 10,000 children from Nazi-dominated Europe who were. He went to work on a farm near Wiveliscombe where conditions were much as they might have been a couple of hundred years before: 'The slatted wooden door led into what appeared to be the only downstairs room with a huge inglenook fireplace . . . Water was taken from a well, cooking was done in [the] fireplace with utensils . . . placed on irons hanging from the chimney over large bundles of twigs brought in from outside

. . . All the water was boiled in a black kettle hung on a hook in the chimney and when we bathed . . . water was heated in large pots in the fireplace.' The boy from an apartment block in Vienna seems to have settled in gamely, but within weeks he suffered a hernia from heaving sheep into the sheep dip and had to go to Minehead hospital.

That was the end of his agricultural trainee experience. When he was discharged Rachel brought him to Golsoncott to convalesce. He then stayed on for a year or so as a kind of general help and handyman, sleeping in a room above the stables, playing the piano in the old nursery, reading back-numbers of *Punch*. Many years later, he provided in his unpublished memoir a fascinating eyewitness account of the household with much of its pre-war infrastructure and ritual still intact.

Then Rachel stepped in again. After leaving school at fourteen, Otto had been apprenticed to a stationery factory back in Vienna. My aunt clearly felt that thought should be given to his long-term future – he was now seventeen – and arranged for him to work as a mill hand down at the paper mill in Watchet.

The small Bristol Channel port has been a centre of industry for a thousand years and more: lime kilns, cloth manufacture, foundries, shipbuilding, rope-making, a flour mill and, since the seventeenth century, the paper mill in which Otto now found himself. The key to Watchet's industrial energy was of course its harbour and its prime site with access to the Bristol Channel shipping routes and the coast of South Wales. Its most thriving years were in the late nineteenth century, when iron-ore mining up on the Brendons was at its peak, with the ore being carried down to Watchet by the mineral line for shipment to the South Wales foundries. But the paper mill too was vitally linked to the port, with freighters bringing pulp from Sweden and coal from Wales and the paper itself being exported by ship. Otto worked eight-hour shifts in one of the several teams overseeing the transformation of huge tubs of slurry into pulp which travelled on belts over steam drying drums, and eventually rolled off as kraft paper.

There he stayed until March 1942 when he achieved his ambition. He joined the British Army, enlisting at Taunton in the Pioneer Corps at the age of eighteen and a half.

Behind this climactic moment in one young life lies the whole confused and complex story of Britain's reception and treatment of so-called 'aliens' in the early years of the war. Otto himself had escaped internment while he was at Golsoncott. In May 1940 the mass internment of Austrian and German refugees began. The initial targets were all males between sixteen and sixty within the southern and eastern coastal belts. Otto, at just sixteen, was technically a potential fifth columnist. In the event, he was put under the supervision of the local constable in Washford, Mr Fish, to whom he had to report regularly. Otto's own explanation of this deft circumvention of the official requirements is that a few quiet words passed between my grandmother and a friend and neighbour of hers who was a local Justice of the Peace. Very likely. As things turned out, Constable Fish and his charge struck up a happy relationship: the policeman was a radio ham with short-wave equipment which he enjoyed demonstrating when Otto reported in. The War Office would have had a fit.

It is one of the oddities of the whole internment process that the War Office was responsible for general internment while the Home Office was responsible for women internees – who were not rounded up until the second wave of internment fever later in 1940. Well before that, Austrian and German refugees had all been classified as enemy aliens and obliged to go before tribunals which sorted them into categories. Those arousing suspicions were placed in Category A, and could be interned. Those considered no risk to national security were assigned to Category C and exempted from restrictions. Refugees not falling into either of these categories – those without the credentials to win them freedom from restrictions but who did not arouse serious doubts – were put into the intermediate Category B, and forbidden to travel more than five miles without police permission.

But the mass internment of the summer of 1940 brushed aside these categories. To be male and of a certain age was enough. The catalyst for this undiscriminating treatment of people, many of whom were themselves victims of the Nazis, was of course the German advance of May and June 1940 and in particular the stories coming out of occupied Holland – the rumours of a Fifth Column already in place, the guerrillas and saboteurs waiting to expedite the invasion. The War Office looked at Britain's refugee population and saw a potential parallel. Public paranoia was whipped up by some sections of the press: 'Intern the lot!' was the cry.

The authorities decided to do precisely that. Contemporary accounts all indicate a headlong and precipitate process. Those who were rounded up felt that they were being unceremoniously hustled out of the way. The sweeps could be as disconcerting as those in a police state. Detectives walked into Hampstead Public Library and announced that all Germans and Austrians present were being taken into custody there and then. Some of the most brutally arbitrary round-ups took place in Whitechapel, Shadwell and Stepney, where East End Jews were taken off to Brixton prison – many of them elderly men who had not been out of London for twenty years. Dr Mallon, the Warden of Toynbee Hall, protested in a letter to *The Times* at this indiscriminate treatment of 'obscure and helpless men about whom the synagogue and their neighbours know all that can be known . . . Surely in the interests of sanity and humanity and the national cause the government will inter- vene.' A peculiarly distasteful corollary to this episode is that some of the men detained in Brixton prison found themselves cheek by jowl with another category of local detainees, British fascists and Nazi sympathizers, who seized on the opportunity for systematic Jew-baiting – kicking and abuse – whenever the prison officers were out of sight.

Most of the internees were sent to the several camps set up for the purpose, of which that on the Isle of Man was the largest. Conditions in all the camps were cramped and uncom- fortable, with a lack of any but minimal communication with family and friends a particular deprivation. In this climate, rumours abounded and depression was prevalent. That said, there is evidence also of an abounding spirit of self-help and improvisation. In some instances 'People's Universities' sprang up, with refugee academics offering classes and lectures. And, famously, three members of the Amadeus Quartet first met in the Isle of Man camp and took advantage of the opportunity to plan and rehearse.

Another major internment camp was at Huyton outside Liverpool, where an unfinished housing estate had been turned into dispiriting billets with no furniture or bedding and nothing but straw sacks to sleep on. It was here that Otto eventually arrived, not as a detainee but as a member of the Pioneer Corps, sent there for three months' basic training.

The opportunity to join the British Army by way of the Pioneer Corps was offered generally to young refugees after August 1940, and taken up by some 2,000, who saw it as a chance to join the war against the Nazis though not, strictly speaking, to fight, since the Pioneer Corps was non-combatant, being effectively the labour force for the Royal Engineers. By this point in late 1940 there was a steady trickle of releases from internment which accelerated until by the middle of 1941 most had been allowed to leave the camps, and some of those sent overseas were permitted to return.

The foreigners in the Pioneer Corps were kept together, segregated from the native recruits, men considered for various reasons unsuitable for active army service. Most of the foreign element would have far outstripped them in capability, to put it baldly. Otto Kun helped to build an ordnance depot near Bicester, in Oxfordshire: he was a navvy on a building site.

Not for long. By 1943 the chance was offered to volunteer for a fighting regiment and thus Otto crossed the Channel in the second wave of the D-Day landings, driving a truck and then a tank in the 7th Armoured Division. He ceased to be Otto Kun and became Douglas Kane. The War Office recommended to Jewish refugees in the army that they should change their names in case they were taken prisoner. The form of Otto's reincarnation seems to have been owed half to my aunt, who suggested a list of names beginning with K, and half to his own admiration for Melvyn Douglas, a popular Hollywood film star of the day.

Otto / Douglas advanced with the British forces through Belgium and into Germany to Hamburg, and served with the Intelligence Corps in the immediate post-war period. He then went into civilian life and a career in the motor industry, eventually establishing his own extremely successful business.

Otto was one of the millions of young Europeans whose lives were entirely directed by the fact of the Third Reich.

History had him by the scruff of the neck. Fifty thousand refugees from the Reich (10,000 of them children) entered Britain between 1933 and 1939, along with another 6,000 from Czechoslovakia. Initially, it was only the relatively prosperous and well-connected who applied for entrance, enabling the British Government to adopt a liberal attitude, but as Nazi persecution intensified the numbers grew. In 1937 several thousand were allowed in, rather defensively described as 'desirable, industrious, intelligent persons' – clearly there was already official nervousness about the prospect of popular resentment of a potential influx. Unemployment was high; this country was already overpopulated and did not have a tradition of immigration. In fact, an insurance policy of sorts was already in place in that every refugee admitted had to be able to name a sponsor providing a financial guarantee. This meant in effect that the only successful applicants were those with friends or relatives in Britain, or those selected by the various refugee organizations active during those years. It was not so much a lottery as a system favouring those able to establish some sort of connection.

There was a certain rationale to the early refusal to give financial assistance to refugees. A blanket provision of resources by the host country could simply be an encouragement to the Reich authorities to strip those in flight of all their wealth even more thoroughly than they were already doing. It was in one sense an attempt – if not very successful – to persuade Germany to permit an orderly migration.

Back then, no one would have believed that the final development of Nazi persecution would be annihilation. Britain's pre-war response to the refugee problem may have been tardy and sometimes confused but it does not compare badly with that of other countries: 136,000 went to the United States, but the quota system continued to be strictly applied, even after the *Anschluss*, with no special relaxation for German and Austrian applicants. Knowing what we now know, the entire exodus seems pitiful in the face of what was to come.

By the summer of 1939 the most compelling kind of refugees were children. Some were already orphaned or homeless. In many more cases, desperate Jewish parents were trying to get their families to safety even if they themselves would be unable to go with them. The Movement for the Care of Children from Germany was formed in November 1938, a response to *Kristallnacht*. The *Kindertransport* began soon after, the first consignment of 320 arriving at Harwich on 2 December. Where possible, children were sponsored by relatives or friends; the majority were guaranteed by the organization itself or locally established committees.

There are many testimonies to this bleak experience. The successive waves of children were held in reception centres initially until more permanent arrangements could be made – bewildered, frightened, separated from their parents. Karen Gershon's synthesis of recollections, *We Came as Children*, is starkly revealing: to read it is to hear dozens of individual voices, creating a tapestry of misery, fortitude, outrage and adaptability. For what shines out is the individuality of each response. All that these children had in common was the refugee experience itself; each dealt with it in their own way. A few were crushed by it, warped for the rest of their lives. Others absorbed their plight, coped, and reinvented themselves. Each and every one, though, must have known that they were now a special order of person: 'I am still a refugee because my roots are where I am not.'

Anyone who is a parent thinks too of those who watched their children go:

From behind the sealed windows I saw my parents again, rigid and unsmiling like two statues, for the last time ever. I was sixteen years old.

I remember the station and everyone was crying and I did not know why. I was seven years old.

. . . the last I ever saw of her was in the Berlin street, outside the friends' house, walking backward along the pavement to get a last look at me, until she rounded the corner and we were parted.

There were five of us – the youngest was not yet two and I was fourteen. We had relations in England and my mother travelled back and forth, rather like a mother-cat transferring her kittens, and parked us wherever she could.

Childhood is itself a continuous process of adaptation and expedient reaction. Given that, the child refugee has a certain advantage over the adult: they retain the capacity to confront extraordinary circumstances with a degree of inborn resilience. Through all the homesickness and wretchedness this stoicism of childhood is apparent in many of the survivors' accounts. Above all, it shows in the ready absorption of a new language. A few of the children clung doggedly and defiantly to German:

I consciously kept my mother-tongue, with the result that I never completely lost my accent in English.

But most moved with ease into another language:

I had forgotten all German by the time I was twelve.

I had to re-learn much of my German when I got a job as translator – my vocabulary was that of a child of eleven.

My German isn't very good . . . The only thing I still do is I count in German.

Sometimes, there is a glimpse into the tragic dislocation of family life effected by the cultural shift:

During the war my granny spent some time with us but it made me unhappy – I had completely dropped German and couldn't converse with her. I could understand every word but was too stubborn and self-conscious to speak it.

When I found after the war that my mother was alive and I started writing to her, I could hardly remember any German and we just wrote to each other now and again.

The refugee and the immigrant are not one and the same, but the situations merge, and provide one of the great human themes of the twentieth century – that of those displaced in time and space. It is the most plangent literary material of our times. From those who have written so vitally about exile in childhood there comes this image of an unreachable past, a perfect and inviolate other world suspended forever within the mind. Eva Hoffman, who went to Canada from her native Poland at the age of fourteen, has called it 'an elsewhere', the lost existence that is nevertheless continually present. That seminal record of childhood, Vladimir Nabokov's *Speak, Memory*, evokes an experience of patrician family life in pre-revolutionary Russia that is the more potent, and the more defiant, in that the historical events that brought it to an end are barely mentioned. Private life is made to float free of public issues. And that is an accurate reflection of how such things appear to the children concerned; just as an ordinary, run-of-the-mill childhood seems at the time to be directed by irrational and unquestionable adult concerns, so the experience of the child at the mercy of the times remains immediate and personal. It is only much later that the dark forces at work become apparent.

We all of us carry through life a kaleidoscopic vision of childhood – a myriad frozen moments. But for those who have known 'an elsewhere' the quality of those moments is different, along with the nature of that other self. I remember an Italian professor of English who told me that he had emigrated with his parents to Italy from Hungary when a small child: 'Somewhere inside me there is a little Hungarian,' he said. And at once I saw him as though with an invisible shadow, a mysteriously alien and unquenchable *alter ego*. When this sense of the shadow presence of other worlds is extended to entire groups and societies the boundaries of time and space seem unreliable. The villages of Bangladesh are shimmering just beyond the pavements of Tower Hamlets, just as once the *shtetls* of Eastern Europe bustled and chattered in the same few acres of London. I can look around at my fellow passengers on a London bus and fancy that half the globe is compressed into that space: private, inaccessible and indestructible.

If I had to select one great fictional creation of the immigrant experience it would probably be Willa Cather's *My Ántonia*. Set in the Midwest in the late nineteenth century, it is *the* great American novel of the pioneering experience, but through its central character and her parents it brilliantly exposes the contrasting possible reactions to immigrant status within one family. The Shimerda family have arrived on the desolate Nebraska prairie from Bohemia, parents and five children, powered by the peasant mother's greed for the promised land. During their first winter of cold, isolation and deprivation, the father commits suicide, desolate for his native Europe and knowing that he can never make peace with this alien place. But he knows too that it is his children – above all his bright bold Ántonia – who can sink roots and make a future. Unable to speak more than a few words of English, he presses a book with two alphabets – English and Bohemian – into the hands of a kindly neighbour and beseeches her: 'Te-e-ach, te-e-ach my Ántonia!' He has seen that language is the key to survival – language and the ability to identify with a new culture. And Ántonia does indeed survive, battling her way through disadvantage to a settled and secure life, mother to a new generation. She is a symbol of the peculiar tenacity and resilience of the European immigrant in America, but she represents too the flexibility and pragmatism of youth as against the cultural rigidity of an older generation. There must be many child immigrants who could identify with Ántonia, rolling up her sleeves to harvest the prairie, robustly negotiating her way into a new society. But retaining always an otherness, that sense of private connection with another time and place.

Flight and dispossession. Set against the eternal stasis of Golsoncott, such traumas seemed entirely incongruous. But a landscape is defined by those who have walked it; a house is given resonance by its inhabitants. When I came to know Golsoncott, the stories of Mary Britnieva and of Otto Kun had become a part of family legend, woven into the complex texture of the place. There was the desk in the study at which Mary had sat while writing her books; when you knew that, the room took on a new significance, packed with event, a silent witness to war and revolution. The curious accord between the two families persisted long into the adult lives of Tsapik and Maria, both of them pitching back at intervals to

Golsoncott for periods of rest and solace, heralded by frantic telegrams and phone calls. Just as their mother's experiences had blown a sharp wind of early twentieth-century reality into the calm of Golsoncott, so the children served up occasional reminders of frenetic lifestyles beyond. My grandmother relished this. She had not the slightest desire to live other than the way in which she did, but the occasional whiff of a breezier climate was invigorating.

The room above the stables in which Otto Kun had spent those months of 1940 fell into disuse soon after. For fifty years it was a pigeon roost, taken over by the flock of white fantails introduced by my grandmother, which had fraternized with the local pigeon population and ended up as speckled hybrids. A few years ago I climbed the collapsing staircase, negotiated the layers of guano and found a rusty iron bedstead. The fifteen-year-old Viennese boy must have lain there, thinking in another language, his head full of images far removed from west Somerset, hearing the same peaceable pigeon rumblings that I heard still. Once again, the place had its secret eloquence, if you knew how to listen: the pigeons were overlaid by darker sounds. And Otto himself, as Douglas Kane, remained in contact with the family for the rest of his life.

The Cedar of Lebanon and Erigeron karvinskianus

Landscape is silent until you unlock the codes. The English landscape with its fields and hedges is just an agreeable and apparently arbitrary patchwork of shape and colour until you know something of its private language. But when those undulations become ridge and furrow, when that die-straight hedgerow is an enclosure boundary, when those lumps and bumps are a deserted medieval village, then the whole place speaks. Cities likewise: brick, stone and glass are merely that until they can be sorted into a chronology, until you know what came before what, until that scrap of wall is sited in its distant century and the curve of that street explained by vanished circumstances.

Gardens, most of all, need interpretation. Stepping out of the veranda door at Golsoncott you looked down into the rose garden and thence beyond its parapet to the sloping lawn below the grass terrace. The great cedar of Lebanon presided over the lawn, which rolled down to the ha-ha. Beyond that, pasture separated the garden proper from the woodland-stream garden and the orchard. Depending on the time of year, you were delighted by the huge pink camellia beside the veranda, the wisteria that draped the house itself, the *Erigeron karvinskianus* that gushed from the walls of the rose garden, the regale lilies, the crimson leaves of *Vitis coignetiae*. If you knew something of garden history you would note the influence of William Robinson (that cedar of Lebanon, the considered but informal effect) and of Gertrude Jekyll (the sunken rose garden with its drystone walls and wide curved stone seat, its lily pond and sundial). Essence of Englishness, you would think, the English garden.

Not so at all. The garden is a cacophony. It is polyglot. It is a global reference system. In fact there is hardly anything here that is English, except for the good offices of Mr Robinson and Miss Jekyll, along with the yew, the primroses, the snowdrops and a handful of other plants.

When I was six I sat in the rose garden making a daisy-chain. It was September 1939. We were living in interesting times, but I was not aware of that. My companion that day was Margaret Reed, also six, whose parents, Tom and Edith, worked at Golsoncott. A photograph shows us brandishing our daisy-chains, looking rather pleased with ourselves. We are sitting amidst the foaming multitude of the pink and white erigeron and our satisfaction is entirely justified. *E. karvinskianus* does not lend itself to daisy-chain-making. It does not have the thick fleshy stem of a meadow daisy but a thin wiry one which requires very precise application of the thumbnail in order to split it effectively. I can recover the experience to this day, the frustration as the thin green wire broke, time after time. *E. karvinskianus* is very much a Gertrude Jekyll planting, almost a Jekyll hallmark, you could say, sparkling down from walls in Jekyll gardens like Hestercombe, softening the hard landscaping and serving as a backdrop to a planting of lilies or groupings of Jekyll silver foliage plants. My grandmother would have taken note, poring over her copy of *Home and Garden*, and hence the plant's pervasive presence at Golsoncott.

An addiction to gardening is, in my view, genetic and in our family runs down the female line. It is now unto the fourth generation, with my daughter Josephine outstripping her forebears by achieving professional qualifications as a garden designer. For me, the most vivid memory shards of childhood have gardens as settings. Those distant, hazy visions of Golsoncott: the black wriggle of tadpoles on water-lily stems, scarlet fuchsia bells, lavender bushes taller than myself. The garden outside Cairo in which I grew up: great eucalyptus trees, plumbago, morning glory, poinsettias. The Alexandria villa gardens in which my parents and I summered: zinnias, bougainvillaea and resident chameleons. And at the heart of it all sit *E. karvinskianus* and the rose garden, where it now seems that the fervour all began.

The family's gardens reflect a hundred years of garden taste. My grandmother's first garden at St Albans had long walks with clipped hedges, island beds in which standard roses were underplanted with white alyssum, formal rose plantings and lawns. By the time she got to Golsoncott, Robinson and Jekyll had stepped in: no more bedding out, with roses as the central feature of a paved and sunken garden brilliant with primroses and jonquils in spring; elsewhere there are informal Robinsonian walks, swathes of snowdrops and bluebells, a tumbling-stream garden with bulrushes and yellow flag irises.

My mother's Egyptian garden made its bow to Robinson by way of a wild and shady water garden with bamboos, papyri, rushes, irises, arum lilies. There was a pergola walk, a lily pond with a weeping willow, a formal avenue of clipped conical evergreens. But there were also geometrical arrangements of beds near to the house, with roses and seasonal plantings. The garden was much admired and considered quintessentially English. My mother even succeeded in growing daffodils, which do not take kindly to north Africa.

By the time the addiction got to me, standards had slumped. The first garden of my married life was behind a Swansea semi-detached. Neither Jack nor I had suspected a dormant gardening gene, but in fact we both had it, and property ownership set it rampant. We fell upon our rectangle of sour turf, matted beds and overgrown shrubs. It was very early spring. All over the place were tender, little rosettes of brilliant green, springing from the decay of winter: certainly something to be cherished. We cleared out a derelict bed and carefully transplanted them, one by one. A few weeks later my grand-mother came to visit. She surveyed our treasured territory with barely concealed dismay. 'I think that if ever I had just a pocket-handkerchief garden I would grow just one thing – really well,' she reflected. Then she turned her attention to our green rosettes. Her dismay was replaced by interested amazement: 'Why have you planted out all that willowherb?'

We learned, over the years and in subsequent gardens. But we were never more than semi-literate, in terms of serious gardening. There was too much else going on, for both of us: gardens were an essential interest and diversion but could never be a central concern. If I were to have my time again, I would be a *real* gardener.

Today, my daughter is creating the heir of the Golsoncott garden, the descendant of her great-grandmother's enterprise. Downsized, once again. It is the garden of the cottage that my grandfather built in 1929, just along the lane, as a home for the Golsoncott gardener. The Reeds lived here; another photo shows Margaret and me swinging on the five-barred entrance gate that is still *in situ*. This is where our family retains a toe-hold in west Somerset, all set for another hundred years, I hope.

Gardening style, eighty years on, in a small country garden for the twenty-first century: the emphasis is on structure and planting. A clever design of curved beds, circular lawns in a figure of eight and embryonic yew hedges divides up a wedge-shaped plot, creates interesting discrete areas and makes the whole thing seem larger. There are a little orchard, gravel paths, planting in swathes of colour – the warm yellows and oranges, the cool blue-and-silver bit. Dramatic use of sculptural plants at focal points – stipa and miscanthus grasses, acanthus. A number of the plants would have been unknown at Golsoncott – all of them popular garden-centre items today and a demonstration of the traditional interdependence of gardening fashion and commercial enterprise. There is *Alchemilla mollis* in abundance, which my grandmother would have relished but apparently did not know. There are euphorbias, hostas, alliums, dicentra, ceanothus – favourites today, though several also feature frequently in Jekyll designs but somehow never reached Golsoncott. The elements of continuity between the two gardens are the aquilegias, self-seeding all over the place, hardy fuchsias, buddleias, hydrangeas, valerian, and the white seat that originated in the St Albans garden and is now nearly a hundred years old. And *Erigeron karvinskianus*, showering from the base of the 'New Dawn' rose over the porch, fingering its way up between cracks in the slate paving.

Like the house, the Golsoncott garden as it once was exists now only in the head. But I can still conjure it up and move around, from space to space, from plant to plant. I can see it, but I now also hear it – as a global mnemonic system. Here we are in west Somerset – lavish green growth, the grey skies from which washes down all that useful rain, the rich pink earth – but much of the rest of the world is here too: the mountains of China and India, Japan, Mexico, South America, Greece, Turkey . . . The garden is both then and now, here and there.

An immense and old wisteria embraced much of the house.

It was probably *W. sinensis*, a native of China whose ubiquitous presence in this country is owed to a tea inspector for the East India Company called John Reeves, who sent it back from Canton in 1816. The Chinese effect on English gardens is pervasive. Golsoncott's Chinese acquisitions, along with the wisteria, included the great pink camellia, the regale lilies banked up against the terrace wall of the rose garden, hydrangeas, iris varieties, acers, *Clematis montana* var. *rubens*, the *Rosa moyesii* bush that cascaded down in the midst of the grassy shrub-rose walk in the kitchen garden. Subtract all of these and the place would have been denuded, would have lost essential character and flavour.

Western plant collectors had their eye on China from the point at which accounts of Chinese gardens began to filter back to Europe by way of Jesuit missionaries. After 1755, foreigners were not allowed to travel into the interior, but plants and seeds still found their way to the West. The camellia arrived in England, along with chrysanthemums, the tree peony and *Hydrangea macrophylla*. Employees of the East India Company like Reeves, based at Canton, Macao and other ports, were crucial in the acquisition process, persuading the captains of tea clippers to find space for plants in tubs and cases. A financial incentive might well have been on offer and, in favoured instances, a naming opportunity, as in the case of Captain Rawes of the *Warren Hastings* immortalized by way of *Camellia reticulata* 'Captain Rawes'. Collectors were indeed driven by the spirit of scientific inquiry, but commercial enterprise was rampant. There was a burgeoning market for cultivated garden rarities and the nurserymen were on to it.

That said, in the early modern period of plant collection (one must remember that introductions had been taking place for hundreds of years) it is the Horticultural Society that leads the way. The group that set up the Society in 1804 – meeting in a room above Hatchards bookshop in Piccadilly – included John Wedgwood, son of Josiah and uncle of Charles Darwin, and the great botanist and discoverer Sir Joseph Banks, by then middle-aged, his circumnavigation of the globe with Captain Cook a distant memory. By 1822 the Society had acquired thirty-three acres at Chiswick on which to establish its own experimental garden. It also set about the dispatch of gardener-collectors around the globe, most significantly to China after 1842, when the treaty ending the Opium Wars between Britain and China meant that the country was at last re-opened to foreigners. Businesslike and entrepreneurial from the outset, the Society would come to dominate the gardening world as the Royal Horticultural Society and, nearly 200 years later, it successfully brings much of central London's traffic to a standstill for the Chelsea Flower Show.

The Horticultural Society sent Robert Fortune to China in 1842 at the suggestion of John Reeves. The existing system of consigning plants back to England in the frequently unreliable hands of tea-clipper captains was unsatisfactory. On a six-month voyage busy seamen had more pressing matters on their minds than watering plants and protecting them against the weather. More plants perished than arrived safely. Clearly, the supervision of skilled gardeners was required. Fortune was a thirty-year-old Scotsman who had recently got the job of superintendent of hothouses at the Society's Chiswick site. He was offered the chance of the China venture and seized it, despite the fact that he had no experience of either voyaging or collecting, and despite the Society's conditions of employment, which were both stringent and miserly. He was to spend a year collecting, with the emphasis on hardy plants and with an eye out in particular for blue peonies and yellow camellias, among other exotica. All that he gathered was to be the property of the Society, though he might acquire some specimens for his own use so long as this was not at the expense of the Society's time. Lest he should run into any difficulties, he was provided with firearms – a fowling piece and pistols – though it had been initially decided that a life-preserver (a lead-weighted stick) would be quite adequate. He would be paid £100 per annum and when he asked for a rise a year later he was told that 'the mere pecuniary returns of your mission ought to be but a secondary consideration to you'.

In the event, Fortune nearly died in the cause of the blue peony (which he never did find, and nor has anyone else) and the firearms proved to be essential baggage. One particularly demanding episode of his travels found him going upriver in a junk which came under attack from five pirate junks, energetically firing broadsides. Fortune coolly held his fire until the pirates came within twenty yards and then let fly (with the fowling piece, one supposes), to devastating effect. He had to repeat this manoeuvre several times more before finally shaking off the enemy. And all this while suffering from a high fever.

There were many further tribulations. He was mugged by angry crowds – foreigners were anathema in China. He barely survived a perilous crossing to the Chusan Islands. He was robbed, mobbed and endured appalling conditions of travel. In one remote spot he very nearly fell into a pit for catching wild boar, from which he would not have been able to extricate himself, thus almost repeating the awful fate of David Douglas, his compatriot collector, who in Hawaii ten years earlier had fallen into a pit and been trampled to death by a wild bullock already trapped there.

So much for plant-collecting as a genteel and leisurely

pastime. The great collectors seem to have shared qualities of youth, tenacity and vigour, along with horticultural skills. Fortune brought 250 plants back from his first Chinese trip, of which a high number survived. He was one of the first collectors to be equipped with Wardian cases, glazed boxes in which plants were kept moist by their own expiration. English gardens owe to him such essential furnishings as winter-flowering jasmine, forsythia (a mixed blessing, given that pervasive yellow rash in spring), weigela, *Viburnum plicatum* and a host of camellias, tree peonies and rhododendrons. All of these carry an invisible freight of another time and another place – mid nineteenth-century China, mysterious, implacable, impenetrable. Rivers hurtle through huge tree-lined gorges. Robert Fortune, wearing Chinese disguise, shares a packed junk with flea-ridden passengers.

In high summer the Golsoncott rose garden was heady with the scent of regale lilies – great stands of them against the terrace wall, with *Erigeron karvinskianus* sparkling away as a backdrop. *Lilium regale* is another native of China, collected by Ernest Wilson at the end of the century. Where Fortune is the early Victorian derring-do explorer, Wilson is the robust Edwardian gentleman traveller. By the time he got to China – aged twenty-three, in 1899 – conditions had improved. He was able to maintain good relations with the Chinese, had no need to resort to disguise, and moved around with an entourage of twenty-five to thirty coolies and two sedan chairs (essential as an indication of status). Nevertheless, the price paid for *L. regale* was high. In 1910, on his fourth trip to China, Wilson travelled to the Min Valley, in the heart of the country, a place of violent climatic extremes, where the lily flourished 'not in twos or threes but in hundreds, in thousands, aye, in tens of thousands . . . for a brief season this Lily transforms a lonely, semi-desert region into a veritable fairyland'. He planned to mark out the site of 6,000 bulbs, to be lifted later in the year, and to this end was negotiating a narrow trail, carried in his sedan chair. Suddenly, there was a rock fall from the precipice above. Wilson leapt from the chair, which was struck by a boulder and sent hurtling down to the river below. He ran for the shelter of an overhanging cliff, where his chair-bearers were already huddled, but failed to make it before he was hit and felled by rocks. His leg was broken in two places. In great pain, he instructed his bearers to make a splint from his camera tripod. During the course of this exercise, a train of mules appeared; since it was impossible to put them into reverse, they had to step over the prostrate Wilson, one by one: 'Then it was that I realized the size of the mule's hoof.' The regale lily, too, takes on a further resonance.

On this trip, Wilson had been sponsored by Professor Sargent of Harvard University's Arnold Arboretum, but his first Chinese venture had been the project of Sir Harry Veitch, of the famous Veitch Nurseries at Coombe Wood. Central to Wilson's brief was the search for *Davidia involucrata* – the handkerchief tree. So many of these expeditions are in pursuit of some botanical holy grail – blue peonies, blue poppies, yellow camellias, white wisteria, the monkey-puzzle tree. Some were found – unfortunately, in the case of the monkey-puzzle, one may think – others never were. The twenty-three-year-old Wilson set out on the davidia hunt armed with a sketch map covering 20,000 square miles, on which was marked the site of a tree spotted some years earlier by a Scottish medical officer posted to the interior. Amazingly, Wilson located it – but reduced to a stump, having been cut down for the building of a house. But his luck turned and soon after he found many hundreds of specimens and was able to secure seeds which were successfully germinated at the Veitch Nurseries. The davidia became one of the gardening trophies of the early twentieth century.

Robert Fortune had introduced 190 species and varieties, the products of his nineteen years of oriental travel. On his later voyages he had shaken off the yoke of the Horticultural Society and was collecting on the side in the service of the East India Company, his principal interest being tea plants. Ernest Wilson eclipses him by a long way, chalking up over 1,000 species: *Clematis armandii*, *Acer griseum*, *Viburnum davidii*, *Magnolia sinensis*, *Clematis montana*, rhododendrons, lilies, peonies, roses, primulas . . . He has furnished the gardens of the nation.

Significantly, it is commercial enterprise that lies behind Wilson's productivity. By the time Sir Harry Veitch targeted the young trainee the Veitch dynasty and their nurseries had dominated British horticulture for nearly a century, regularly employing and dispatching trained plant collectors around the world. They had competitors, but were undoubted market leaders until the demise of the firm. Their handsome catalogues are a chart to the contents of Victorian and Edwardian gardens.

The concept of the garden is ancient and compelling – the recognition that nature is beautiful but to be manipulated, that it can benefit from human intervention. Gardening is probably the most widespread form of creativity – subject of course to the winds of fashion and the dictates of commerce – a way in which innumerable people display their particular taste and choice. Gardening is a private and personal activity, but gardens can be public, portentous and expressions of social standing in the same way as architecture. Lancelot Brown's wholesale reconstructions of landscape in the eighteenth century are a far cry from the individualities of the twentieth-century back garden, but there is a flicker of the same spirit at work – the notion that the status quo might be improved upon. But equally as powerful as someone's contribution is the invisible baggage that any garden carries, all those direct-ives from elsewhere. What we plant and how we plant it are up to us, but much has already been decided, not just by soil and climate, but by what has been done at other times, by people of whom we know little or nothing.

Below the Golsoncott veranda and above the rose garden were two long beds. Here, my grandmother clung to the outdated practice of bedding out. These were the dahlia gar-dens: tall, staked cactus dahlias at the back, the smaller free-flowering varieties in front, both single and pom-pom. I doubt if she had ever heard of the explorer Alexander von Humboldt, and Mexico was not high on her agenda of interests, but it is from there that Humboldt sent back dahlia seed in 1804. And Mexico fingered her garden again a few paces on, as you went through the low wrought-iron gate at the end of the dahlia-border path and down the little flight of steps on to the terrace between the canal garden, hidden behind its high yew hedges, and the further steps down on to the tennis lawn. Nearby were huge old choisya bushes, their leaves smelling of orange when you crushed them, smothered in white flowers in spring.

Turning your back on the choisya bushes, you looked down into the Japanese-maple garden, an enclosed grassy area divided from the rose garden by another wrought-iron gate and shaded by several fine acers planted when the garden was laid out. I don't know which species these were but I remember one with leaves pouring to the ground, like a feathered scarlet mantle, and the effect of sunlight sifting down through a canopy of green, bronze and gold. Both Fortune and Wilson were active in Japan as well as in China. Japanese flora was as renowned as that of China and equally inaccessible for centuries, but by the first half of the nineteenth century Japanese plants were filtering back to Europe – bamboos, lilies, azaleas, camellias and hydrangeas (including *H. paniculata*, a particular pride and joy of my grandmother's amid her great sweep of hydrangeas in front of the house). Wilson went to Japan with the collection of cherries as his main objective, but it is to Sir James Veitch – last of the nurseries dynasty – that we owe the (mixed) blessing of the omnipresent double-flowered cherries that send a pink tide across every suburb in spring. Like the forsythia, they can be too much with us.

Once through the maple garden, the grass terrace below the rose garden was to your left, reaching away to the cedar summer house fronted by huge bushes of old English lavender (something native, at last), with climbing and rambling roses all over the wall. To the right was the high hedge around the tennis lawn and in front was the lawn itself, sloping gently down to the ha-ha. The cedar of Lebanon dominated here. Obvious enough where that comes from, and in fact it has a long history in this country, listed in Sir Thomas Hanmer's *Garden Book* of 1659, though it may not have been widely known until later. This magnificent tree was a William Robinson favourite, 'perhaps the finest evergreen tree ever brought to our country and as hardy as our own trees. If we use evergreen trees they ought to be the noblest and the hardiest.' He advocated planting cedars 'massed in groups', as they grow in their native land, thus protected against wind. A nice idea but one that supposes a considerable acreage – I can see why my grandmother restricted herself to a single specimen, which occupied much of the lawn in its prime. Visiting children traditionally climbed it, and equally traditionally got stuck and had to be rescued with ladders.

A steep bank fell away from the tennis lawn yew hedge (native again, for a change) and with this we are in South America. Huge tumbling bushes of *Fuchsia magellanica*, both the scarlet and the pink varieties. This profuse and glorious creature loves the mild, damp weather of the West Country, as do its descendants, the many hybrids bred in the nineteenth century, when the slender and dainty flower of *F. magellanica* was reborn with ruffles, frills, great waxy corollas and extravagant colour combinations.

Below the fuchsia bank there were swathes of naturalized narcissi. Several different varieties, with an emphasis on the smaller, free-flowering kinds. No strident 'King Alfred'. And with these we are in Europe at last, with various species originating in Spain, Portugal and the Maritime Alps. Many were collected in the nineteenth century by an energetic Scot called Peter Barr (Scotland's contribution to plant-collecting has been phenomenal) who had set out to rediscover as many as possible of the species listed in a plant catalogue of 1629 and subsequently lost. All these botanical transitions conjure up vibrant pictures – Wilson's thousands of regale lilies lighting up the Chinese gorge, the sad stump of that chopped-down davidia – but perhaps none is more poignant than the fate of the narcissus. Once blowing wild and free on southern European hillsides (where some, of course, still do), now reincarnated as the staple plant of every British garden, patio, window-box and public park. It has been hybridized out of all recognition, in many cases. Moreover, bulb collection has been one of the more dubious areas of acquisition. One particular white daffodil, *Narcissus alpestris*, a rare plant of the Pyrenees, was collected virtually to extinction in the early part of the twentieth century. One thinks uneasily of Wilson and his targeted 6,000 *Lillium regale*. What did that valley look like after he'd had his way with it?

The Golsoncott garden was a sloping site, falling away from the back of the house and with its varying levels cleverly exploited. A steep little flight of steps led up from the tennis lawn to the wide terrace separating it from the canal garden. This sheltered and sunny place was home to the peonies – a long border of them underplanted with more narcissi. China muscling in again, depending on variety – all I remember is the great pink blowsy explosion of high summer. China would have supplied the white buddleias that fringed the steps up to the gap in the yew hedge and the entrance to the canal garden. But my grandmother's favoured silver leaf plants (influence of Jekyll, again, but all of them going strong today) are a wave in a different direction, with *Cineraria maritima* emanating from Australia and the South Sea Islands and *Senecio laxifolius* from New Zealand. And the flowering currant by the kitchen garden gate – *Ribes sanguineum* – is a native of western America, introduced by another of those intrepid Scots, David Douglas. Douglas had been apprenticed as a gardener at the age of eleven and while working at the Botanic Gardens in Glasgow as a young man came to the attention of Sir William Hooker (later to be the first Director of Kew). Hooker took him up and put his name forward as a collector for the Horticultural Society. Thus, in 1823 Douglas was sent to North America, the first of several voyages. He is very much in the Fortune tradition – intrepid and adventurous, hardened by his experience roaming the Scottish Highlands, happy to live rough and undaunted by the wild terrain and fast-flowing rivers of the area around Fort Vancouver, where he spent much time. He had brushes with grizzly bears and Native Americans, though he was astute enough to get on good terms with the latter whenever he could and to make use of their knowledge of plants and habitats. Apart from the homely flowering currant, he is remembered in the Douglas fir, along with *Garrya elliptica* and a good deal more.

There was one corner of the canal garden that was forever England. The long narrow area was entirely enclosed by high yew hedges. One end met up with the curved veranda of what would today be called a conservatory but was known at Golsoncott as the sun parlour. Wisteria dripped down from this, reflected in the square pond from which opened the canal, a couple of feet wide, running the length of the garden to a matching square pond at the other end. Here were the snowdrops – vast swathes and drifts so well established that they probed out into the long beds below the hedges, where they were not supposed to be and which were given over to irises.

The iris garden, this was: many varieties, horribly labour-intensive. I can see my grandmother now, doggedly weeding and dividing, in her sixties, seventies, eighties. There were many different kinds, so they could have had their origins around the whole globe – China, Japan, North America, Turkey, Morocco . . . Most bearded irises are the products of hybridization, and my grandmother grew a fair number of those, which have to be considered of no fixed abode, I suppose. The square ponds at both ends and at the centre of the canal had stands of blue bulrushes, and there were water lilies everywhere. Glimmering between the water-lily pads were goldfish – oriental no doubt. And munching on the green weed at the sides were droves of tadpoles, very definitely native.

Beyond the high yew hedge of the iris garden was the kitchen garden, a rectangular site of about half an acre, sloping up to a brick wall that supported a line of ancient plums. The archetypal kitchen garden, it now seems. A place that you could slowly nibble your way around, in high summer: the forest of raspberry canes, including the rare and succulent yellow variety; huge juicy ruby gooseberries; crisp raw peas; last year's apples, stacked away on shelves in the gloriously aromatic apple house; plums, golden-fleshed Victorias, small sharp purple ones; sun-warm tomatoes from the greenhouse, with yellow ones again a speciality.

This was also the source of flowers for the house. Ranks of dahlias and chrysanthemums for cutting, a cliff of sweet peas. There were exuberant stands of mint, rosemary bushes, mounds of thyme. You pinched and sniffed as much as you nibbled. A deeply sensual place, the kitchen garden, everything going to extremes, it seemed – the great swags of apples on the lines of espaliers that flanked the central path, the rampant banks of potatoes, plumes of asparagus.

It had its dark privacy, also – the gardener's potting shed, into which one must not go. Through the open door there was the glimpse of a battered wicker armchair with earth-stained cushion, a shelf with tins of tobacco, a thermos, newspapers. And to the door were pinned the shrivelled and mummified corpses of moles, like a gamekeeper's gibbet – *pour encourager les autres*, I suppose.

Any garden is a combination of structure and furnishings. Golsoncott owed its furnishings to the distant efforts of those who have roamed the globe in search of plants, driven by scientific curiosity, commercial zest or a combination of the two. To think of this is to see the place overlaid by images of other times and other worlds. All these botanical immigrants, so familiar, so apparently domestic, assume a compelling new presence. They are strangers in our midst, with a tale to tell.

And amongst them roam shadowy figures, stereotyped by their era, because that is the only way in which we can see them. Buttoned into stiff Victorian costumes, or tricked out in seventeenth-century gear like John Tradescant the Younger, who brought from Virginia the *Aquilegia canadensis*, which shot up all over the place, as briskly Somerset as the primroses, you would think.

The structure of the place was rooted in its own time, with concessions to elsewhere. The most significant gesture was the ha-ha, providing a four-foot drop from the lawn to the pasture beyond, where horses or cattle grazed. The ha-ha is a country-mansion device, and Golsoncott was not that, so there was an element of aspiration or ambition about it, but also practicality. It kept the animals out of the garden, and allowed the view from the veranda and the rose-garden terrace to sweep away down to the copse and the stream garden without the intrusion of a hedge or wall. One theory about the origins of the ha-ha has it derived from the military defensive system of a ditch dug in front of a hedge or fortification. As for its name, this is the explanation given by the author of the influential *La Théorie et la pratique du jardinage*, published by A. J. Dezallier d'Argenville in 1709 and translated into English by John James shortly after:

At present we frequently make through views, called *Ah, Ahs*, which are openings in the walls [of the garden], without grilles, to the very level of the walks, with a large and deep ditch at the foot of them, lined on both sides to sustain the earth, and prevent the getting over, which surprises the eye on coming near it, and makes one cry *Ah! Ah!* whence it gets its name.

Absurd but persuasive.

The stock feature of the seventeenth-century grand garden was the parterre giving way to a vista. There was an echo of that at Golsoncott: the rose garden was not a parterre, but it played the part of the formal area adjacent to the house, beyond which an open space leads the eye away towards the distance. The basic geometry of power-gardening lingered on long after the emphasis of garden design had turned towards the demands of humbler acreages. The Victorian building boom created hundreds of thousands of new gardens, along with a middle-class clientele keen to embellish their personal space. John Loudon's *The Suburban Gardener and Villa Companion* of 1838 targets this new concept in gardening – the very title is wonderfully emotive. He is advocating the charms of existing gardens rather than offering original designs, but classifies garden styles succinctly into picturesque, gardenesque and rustic. Picturesque harked back to the eighteenth-century stately home vision – the manipulation of natural scenery into 'that particularly suitable for being represented by painting'. Gardenesque was a new and apt term, implying garden design calculated to display to their best individual trees, shrubs and plants, along with attention to such features as smooth green lawns and well-constructed paths and walks. Rustic is the natural look displayed by the gardens of labourers' cottages. In this last, and in the fact that he saw it as an appropriate style for introduction into the gardens of the gentry, Loudon is anticipating William Robinson, who could be little short of ecstatic about cottage gardening.

Golsoncott had a whiff of all three forms, I now see, along with its touch of *folie de grandeur* by way of the ha-ha. Today, much garden taste is directed by television programmes; enthusiastic thirty-somethings exhort from the screen and have the nation rushing into its back garden to paint the fence purple, slap down some decking, create a water feature. Eighty years ago, my grandmother would have been directed by *Country Life*, garden books, and what she saw around her. But also by the accretions of garden practice, which declared that you could not hold up your head in polite gardening society without a good lawn, a rose garden, seasonal bedding, a herbaceous border, and maybe a pergola and a lily pond if you were in serious competition.

My grandmother installed some of these features at Golsoncott but above all she turned to Robinson and Jekyll. I know she did, because we have her copies of their books. Her edition of Robinson's *The English Flower Garden* is the 1889 seventh edition (the first edition was 1883). It is somewhat the worse for wear now, as well it might be after a hundred years, a fine gold-tooled poppy on the front of its dark-blue binding, and within a pungent combination of swingeing opinions, confident and persuasive advocacy of the Robinsonian theory of gardening, and vigorous practical advice. The one quality that garden writers seem to have in common is an implacable self-confidence, rising to didacticism. One cannot but feel that Robinson set the pace. And why not? If you have strong views and a determination to transmit them, you will get nowhere with understatement. Robinson saw all around him the rigidities of Victorian gardening, the formality derived from Sir Joseph Paxton and others, the obsession with bedding out – 'pastry-work gardening' – and the whole Crystal Palace style. He was not categorically opposed to seasonal planting; his bugbear was the admired high Victorian expression of the form:

Only scarlet Geraniums, yellow Calceolarias, blue Lobelias, or purple Verbenas were used; and the following year, by way of a change, there were Verbenas, Calceolarias, and Geraniums, – the constant repetition of this scarlet, yellow, and blue nauseating even those with little taste in gardening matters, whilst those with finer perceptions began to inquire for the Parsley bed, by way of relief.

The system thrives yet today, of course, in municipal gardening, and can be studied up and down the country in parks, memorial gardens and on seafronts and urban roundabouts.

Robinson was born in Ireland in 1838 and was foreman in the gardens of Ballykilcavan, Stradbally, by the time he was twenty-one. But he was soon over in England, working in the Royal Botanic Society's gardens at Regent's Park. Here he was in charge of the herbaceous section but also, significantly, responsible for a wild garden, in the service of which he got to know native plants and how they appear in the wild, along with cottage garden practices. It was this experience and observation that was crucial to the formation of his taste for the natural look:

I saw the flower gardener meanly trying to rival the tile or wallpaper men, and throwing aside with contempt all the lovely things that through their height or form did not conform . . . And so I began to see clearly that the common way was a great error and the greatest obstacle to true gardening or artistic effects of any kind in the flower garden or home landscape, and then made up my mind to fight the thing in any way open to me.

Into battle. Robinson's initial weapon was his weekly journal the *Garden*, into which he sunk all his savings. And, crucially, it was through this that he met Gertrude Jekyll, who became one of the contributors. The combination of their views and talents would determine the nature of gardening in these islands for decades to come.

Jekyll wrote the chapter on 'Colour in the Flower Garden' in *The English Flower Garden*. There were other collaborators, but the robust tone of the book comes from Robinson himself. Here he set out his theory of gardening – 'the best kind of garden should arise out of its site and conditions as happily as a primrose out of a cool bank'. He told his readers how to do it and equally how not to do it, as specified in combative chapter heads: 'AGAINST STYLES, USELESS STONEWORK, AND STEREOTYPED PLANS', 'USE IN THE GARDEN OF BUILDERS, AND OTHER DEGRADED FORMS OF THE PLAS-TIC ART'. He cited and illustrated existing grand gardens that demonstrated the various points he was making, and identified very precisely what you should plant where, if you were planning to toe the Robinsonian line. Armed with *The English Flower Garden*, you could put your own domain on the cutting edge of *fin-de-siècle* horticultural style.

But a domain it had better be. Robinson's proposals demand space. Despite his fervent championship of the cottage garden style, his eye is on wide acres, not the suburban and villa gardens envisaged by Loudon (of whom he much approved, seeing the latter's more enlightened style as having been quenched and sidelined by the Paxton school). The more patrician gardener could learn from the 'rustic' use of informal groupings, climbing roses against house walls, old country favourites like hollyhocks, larkspur and lupins. The ideal Robinsonian garden required plenty of room – for those wide grassy walks with swathes of spring bulbs, the tree groupings, the great borders of herbaceous plants and shrubs, the sweep-ing lawns and, above all, for those wild gardens, which might be woodland areas, or broad stretches of grassland with specimen trees and naturalized plantings. The wild garden was a brave new concept, back then; at the beginning of this century it is in the forefront of garden fashion, fitting in nicely with environmental and ecological concerns and the gardening good taste that favours the small-flowered, delicate and miniature and abhors all that is large, double, heftily trumpeted or smothered in blossom. It is instructive to watch those television garden gurus determinedly trying to cram a wild garden into the toe of a fifty-foot suburban plot.

Gertrude Jekyll is altogether more temperate than Robinson. Indeed, her contribution to the debate over design and formality versus plantsmanship and artistry was to inject the voice of sweet reason. You could make use of both. Robinson became locked into an ideological battle with Reginald Blomfield, whose publication of *The Formal Garden in England* in 1892 was a calculated challenge to Robinsonian theories. Blomfield argued for the essential role of architecture in garden design, with the horticulturist as merely the servant of the designer; 'landscape gardening' he dismissed as an ineffectual manipulation of nature. Robinson's *The English Flower Garden* is full of diatribes about the intrusive role of the architect in gardening. Polarized positions, with no room for compromise, and nicely illustrative of the state that garden theorists can get themselves into when the blood is up. Jekyll brought sanity to the situation by developing a philosophy of gardening which incorporated the best of Robinsonian ideas but also emphasized the essential partnership between overall design and architectural elements – the hard landscaping, they call it nowadays – and the skill and knowledge of the horticulturalist.

Gertrude Jekyll is the epitome of the indomitable and unstoppable late Victorian woman. Photographs show a small, dumpy person – unassuming but, one senses, formidable. Born in 1843, she studied at the South Kensington School of Art, where she came under the influence of William Morris, and formed a strong affinity with the Arts and Crafts Movement. And indeed she was always an artist first and foremost – or maybe craftswoman is the better term – bringing to the disposition of plants and the structure of a garden her distinctive eye for colour and form. She was a colourist by instinct; the emphasis is on colour groupings and gradations in the 250 garden plans that she drew up during her heyday as an esteemed garden consultant – one hesitates to use the word designer since she never referred to the activity as anything but gardening. She was a plantswoman *par excellence*, and while she did indeed have a range of favourites, some of which have become hallmarks of Jekyll style, the image of a palette devoted entirely to soft pinks and blues, or the white and silver combination, is a misrepresentation. She used strong colours with relish; the planting schemes for her gardens are warm with yellows and reds. The point was colour combination and gradation, along with shrewd attention to the architecture of plants themselves: soft mounds of clipped santolina, the shapely frame of tall eryngiums. And an insistence above all on the successful marriage of plant and setting.

Jekyll's association with Robinson was productive, but perhaps even more so was her collaboration with Edwin Lutyens. She met the architect in 1889, when he was only twenty and she was in her mid-forties. There seems to have been instant empathy between them, based on a shared passion for traditional craftsmanship and materials, and the vernacular building styles of the Surrey landscape in which Jekyll was now living and where she created her own garden at Munstead Wood, complemented eventually by the house that Lutyens designed for her. Her popular and influential book, *Home and*

Garden, rushes off into enthusiastic digressions on the virtues of cottage architecture, or on the appeal of an old stone bridge. She is interested in the harmony between plants and natural materials; a photograph in the book of the paved and cobbled path in front of a row of cottages, with a wooden water-butt and plants tumbling from the walls, is a hint of things to come, when Lutyens's elegant steps, balustrades and drystone walls would serve as foils for her plantings.

The Jekyll influence was all over the place at Golsoncott. Lutyens too. The house was not a Lutyens design, but it could well have been, with its rusticated stone pillars on the veranda, its leaded casement windows, its overhanging tiled roof. Very much of its time, very much 'Surrey school'. And outside one could well think that the distinguished partnership had been at work. The sunken rose garden could be a Lutyens layout, while its furnishings – the regale lilies, the *Erigeron karvin-skianus* and hart's-tongue ferns and *Corydalis ochroleuca* springing from the walls, the sisyrinchiums clustered in cracks of the paving, the primroses and the *Anemone blanda*, were all the stuff of a Jekyll plan. Here, for fifty years, my grandmother battled with black spot on the roses and took ceremonial photographs of visiting relations and their new babies, perhaps occasionally beaming an appreciative thought towards those who had inspired the place. Elsewhere, the long canal in the iris garden was an almost exact replica of the Jekyll design of a rill garden in the Deanery in Sonning, Berkshire. And the summer house, the potting sheds and the apple store were all of silvery wood with overlapping boards, nicely vernacular.

Home and Garden was first published in 1900. Jekyll's voice is very different from Robinson's; the confidence is there, but not the didacticism or the note of combat. The style is personal, and distinctly rambling. She describes the building of her own house, and the studied craftsmanship involved. She devotes pages to rapturous but intense observation of the natural growth of a local wood, an odd combination of a precise botanical scrutiny with an outburst of anthropomorphism when she has an oak making a heroic sacrifice for a chestnut being strangled by a honeysuckle – 'Neighbour, throw out a little branch and send me the enemy. I am doomed already; a little more can only bring the end somewhat sooner . . .' There is an account of the workshop in which she did her craft work, surveys of her own garden with detailed and specific suggestions for similar plantings. And then there is an entire chapter on her cats, including instructions on how to give a 'pussies' tea-party' for a nine-year-old niece: 'First a thick strip of fish was laid right across each saucer; an equal strip of cold rice-pudding met it transversely, forming a cross-shaped figure that left four spaces in the angles. Thick cream was poured into these spaces . . .' That austere and somewhat daunting figure of the photographs suddenly looks different. Children crop up again in the chapter on how to make pot-pourri. Get hold of any children that come to hand, the reader is told, and set them to work gathering rose petals. There follow precise and elaborate directions on how to lay down the stuff on what sounds like an industrial scale, filling fifteen-gallon oak casks from complex recipes that vary according to the species of rose used.

Home and Garden must have directed the activities of many an Edwardian housewife – and on, indeed, into the twenties and thirties when my grandmother was certainly using it. Her own flower arrangements were very much in the style of Jekyll's elegant creations as featured in the illustrative photographs. It is a beguiling and discursive book (any offer of an editorial hand rejected, one suspects) but also practical, and has to be seen as the forerunner of the later torrent of publications aimed at the aspiring middle-class home owner, and a distant ancestor of the glossy 'lifestyle' books that are the staple of every bookshop today.

The Golsoncott garden now floats free of time and space – preserved in the mind's eye, eloquent of elsewhere and of people who never knew it. But gardening as an activity has always seemed to me to defy the domination of the present. Digging, planting and planning, you move ahead, and look back. My own gardening days are done, but the crispest pleasure that I remember is that interesting sense of displacement. Sorting bulbs on an autumn afternoon – shiny brown tulips, the papery cluster of narcissi, the white teardrops of dwarf iris – you were both here and now but also projected forward into another season, when these things would have undergone their miraculous metamorphosis. Poring over the vibrant pages of a new seed catalogue, you were designing the summer to come – while scribbled notes in last year's catalogues warned against the failures and the misplaced choices. And the seeds themselves were both a sensual delight – glossy pellets, parachutes, thistledown, tiny cuttlefish, flakes, spears, golden dust – and also amazing hostages to the future. Sowing seed in the greenhouse was an act of faith: the ritual of the seed trays, the tactile compost, the blank inviting markers and the special pen was like the performance of some religious office, the invocation of an event that was both impossible and entirely reliable. The seeds were the guarantee of the turning of the world, their strange disguises a coded account of the colour and the exuberance to come.

As an activity, gardening is a combination of immediacy and imaginative projection. Perhaps that is why it is so satisfying – a fusion of physical endeavour with a dream of things to come.

A garden is perilously unstable. A few decades of neglect and it melts into the landscape, its existence to be read only by the perceptive. It becomes archaeology, with some tenacious growths hinting at what once was there. Gardeners know this; the fragility of the present is set against the robustness of digging and planting, the emphatic qualities of earth and roots and stems. To garden is to seize the day.

The Sunset Painting and the Harness Room

Above the sideboard in the dining-room there hung a painting by the late Victorian artist B. W. Leader. I always thought of it simply as the sunset picture, and in my romantic years – fourteen through about seventeen – it expressed everything I felt about the country. It was a landscape with a farmhouse and trees; small figures wander along a muddy track towards the farmhouse, where other figures wait in apparent welcome. The whole picture is suffused with light from a rich roseate sky, which is reflected in pools of water in the foreground. The trees are shapely, the detail is precise. You could step into that painting, smell the grass, feel the breeze, walk away into that sunset. A celebration of the countryside, with the suggestion of a tranquil home – and it is a most glorious evening. As a painting, it is a neat instance of the way in which art can condition emotion and response.

West Somerset has crept much closer to London than it was in the 1920s. It was still a long way away in the 1950s. I remember the all-day car journey, with the picnic basket in the boot and the stops for lunch and tea. A whisk up the M5 and the M4, today, and you're in London. The country was further from the town, in every sense; rural and urban life were appositions. They still are, but not in quite that style of mutual exclusion.

My grandmother went to London once or twice a year, in full fig – fur coat, best hat – and with all her reservations about 'town' working overtime. A couple of days would be spent doing essential shopping, paying visits and taking in a play. After which, prejudices satisfactorily confirmed (the noise, the dirt, the crowds . . .), she withdrew to the civilized world, whence she pressed offers of temporary sanctuary upon family and friends condemned to live an urban life.

In adolescence, my view of town and country was one of stark contrast – a polarity imbued moreover with moral and aesthetic significance. Country was good; town was bad. Country was healthy, beautiful, inspirational and a solace to the soul; town was dirty, ugly, corruptive and dulled the senses. This vision owed a good deal to my grandmother, of course, but it was also a reflection of much received opinion of the time – and indeed of times before and since. It was derived from art and literature, an insidious conditioning that had affected my childhood perception even in distant Egypt, where the classic English divide was unthinkable and unknown. I had been born in Cairo and was growing up there; England was a place last visited when I was six. I knew that it was apparently the centre of the universe, a nirvana of mysterious and unparalleled quality, and that one must feel towards it an unqualified loyalty and affection – though quite how to do this was always something of a puzzle when all one had to focus on were a hazy concept of greenery, a King and Queen, and a distinctive flag which must not be flown the wrong way up. It was evidently a place of diverse appearances (I'd read and seen enough to know that): Phiz and Cruikshank illustrations to Dickens, Shell posters, the nursery calendar on which snow and robins gave way to meadows of gambolling lambs, Alison Utley and Beatrix Potter and Arthur Rackham and Kate Greenaway. But it was clear to me which were the valued aspects, what it was that sent people all misty-eyed and reverent: green fields, babbling brooks, thatched cottages, primroses and bluebell woods. I learned Tennyson by heart – 'I come from haunts of coot and hern . . .' – and tried to get misty myself.

When I returned to the fabled land, aged twelve, prejudices were already set. Shunted between my London and Somerset grandmothers, I knew where I was best off. Never mind that a small voice whispered sedition about the city: interesting, it said . . . busy, bright, bustling, it said . . . shops, cinemas, people, fun. But right-minded folk settled for country life, didn't they?

A part of me still believes that. I am a city dweller now, because needs must, but it doesn't feel quite right. It suits me well enough, but an atavistic instinct tells me that something is awry. Partly, this is indeed inclination – a hunger for space, a horizon, things growing, sky and weather – but it is also a cultural conditioning, an unconscious imperative.

We all led rural lives, time was; most of us are descended from peasants. The demographic history of this country records a gradual leeching of population away from the fields and into the towns. A computer simulation of the process would show the cities expanding, sprawling, spreading like a rash in the North and the Midlands, joining up and merging into conglomerate urban masses. The Roman towns were tiny islands amid the enveloping green, but potent signals of the way things would go. Economic circumstance cracks the whip and, century by century, the trickle becomes a steady stream and eventually a torrent until, by the beginning of the twentieth century, nearly 80 per cent of the population are living in towns. A rural world has become an urban and industrial one; most people wake every morning amid smoke, brick, and concentrated humanity.

But at that point a high proportion of Britons were only

one or two generations removed from the land – folk memory of it was still strong. The accelerated flood into the towns, cities and above all the new industrial conurbations took place during the nineteenth century. Our great-great-great grandparents, or thereabouts. Near enough for there to be some cerebral link, but so far removed for reality to undergo a sea-change into some kind of mythology. The notion of Arcadia is born – the place for which we yearn, the ideal world in which we should really be. In the process of metamorphosis the brute facts become submerged: the grim truth of existence in a thatched cottage – the punishing labour, the cold, the hunger, the lives chopped short. That long-ago and faraway place has achieved the imperishable glow of nostalgia. It has prompted all those aspirations – the weekend retreat, the retirement home tucked away up a lane. Or, on a simpler scale, the drive out into the country just to check that it is still there, still carrying on as it should. Somewhere in all this there is perhaps a glimmer of genuine ancestral feeling. People do not on the whole abandon a traditional and established way of life except out of necessity. The flight from the land to the differently harsh circumstances of industrial Britain happened because many were impelled to look for work or believed that things might be more endurable elsewhere. Most would have stayed put, given adequate opportunities where they were.

Migration becomes dispossession, as the mythology takes form. Several generations on, those born and bred to the city have now this fantasized vision of that alternative world. They may not necessarily want to be there, except for the occasional jaunt. Remember those London evacuee mothers who beat it back to the East End as soon as they could. But an aesthetic has been established, fortified by art and literature, by advertising, by consumer goods. In the 1930s, aertex-shirted hikers smile from London Transport posters, leaning on stiles with a backdrop of blue sky and fleecy clouds. By the 1970s, we are sprigged out in Laura Ashley fabrics, eating wholemeal bread, hanging corn dollies from our stripped-pine dressers; petrol advertisements show happy families romping through dappled woods, latest-model cars whisk along empty roads amid exquisite scenery. The country has become very near: turn off the motorway and you've arrived. You can bring it into your own home, nicely sanitized – its essence is easily available in supermarkets and department stores. The brute contrast of the 1900s is a thing of the past, or so it seems. There is no longer that mutual exclusion. Every city child knows what size a cow is, now; we all listen to *The Archers* and watch vet programmes. The country is our birthright; it belongs to us all and plenty of us have a sneaking feeling that that's where we ought to be.

But there is a paradox here. The creation of Arcadia has also widened the chasm between town and country. The image of rural life is accessible; there is a sense in which we can live a proxy rural life from the city centre, nowadays. But those who actually live in Arcadia – above all those who still grub a living from it – don't see things in quite the same way. For them, reality can be a contemporary version of the deprivations of another century: unemployment, low wages, inadequate facilities, absence of choice. The summer influx of voyeurs may mean economic salvation for some, but it is also a reminder that we are two nations.

Golsoncott had a mere toe-hold on agricultural economy: my aunt kept some Devon red polls, for marketing purposes, and a crop of hay was taken from the top field. But she and my grandmother were quite clear about their alignment. 'Trippers!' my grandmother would snort, confronted by a

car-load of holiday visitors in the lane; she would sit behind
the driving wheel with a basilisk stare, forcing them to back
to the nearest passing place. Locals have right of way. When
an incomer who had bought a nearby cottage made the terrible
gaffe of grumbling to Rachel because a farm trailer had spilled
manure near his gate, he was silently ostracized. My grandmother's attitude towards west Somerset was one of uncom-
promising patriotism; nowhere else matched up for natural
beauty and the sterling qualities of its inhabitants, though she
would concede that the South Hams in Devon were quite
pretty. Arcadia indeed, but a down-to-earth Arcadia of mud,
muck and weather.

There was a copy of *Tarka the Otter* at Golsoncott. Summer
reading for me on the veranda, once again, aged fourteen or
so. There was also *Bevis, The Story of a Boy*, and works by Mary
Webb and W. H. Hudson. The household had never been
a bookish one; what was on the shelves represented stock
middle-brow reading of the 1920s and 1930s, and as such tapped
in with a vengeance to the literary taste for the romanticization
of rural life. I read Mary Webb – *Precious Bane* and so forth –
with interest but some perplexity, looking with new eyes at
those around me. Could the private life of a Somerset hamlet
be like this? I had met up with Mary Webb before, on my
parents' shelves in Egypt, and had been even more bewildered.
Some years later, coming across *Cold Comfort Farm*, I realized
with the glee of revelation what was going on here. Oh, the
sukebind, the sukebind . . . A country spring would never be
the same again.

Literature has a lot to answer for, where concepts of the
countryside are concerned. Thomas Hardy, of course, but
crucially also the animistic school exemplified by W. H.
Hudson, who saw the natural world as the source of mystical

solace, a lost paradise reflecting the irretrievable animality of childhood: 'The return to an instinctive or primitive state of mind is accompanied by this feeling of elation, which, in the very young, rises to an intense gladness, and sometimes makes them mad with joy, like animals newly escaped from captivity.' Rima, the heroine of *Green Mansions*, is just such a primitive free spirit. Childish rather than child-like, one may think; I find the book quite unreadable now, but to dip into it is to receive an eerie echo of early reading affinities – at fifteen I was enthralled. More palatable is *A Shepherd's Life* – a eulogy of nature and the simple peasant lot on the Wiltshire Downs in the early 1900s.

Richard Jefferies, publishing in the 1880s and 1890s, is the great popularizer of nature and rural life. *Bevis* was a huge best-seller and still very much around in the 1920s and 1930s; a generation grew up on that vision of a boyhood fantasy world amid an idyllic countryside. Again, the climate seems uncomfortably mawkish now, though the nature stuff interestingly evokes a landscape not yet blasted by pesticides and intensive farming. And *The Toilers of the Field* brings the same qualities of precise observation to bear on the lifestyle of the Edwardian farm labourer, serving up an almost sociological account. There was a copy of Jefferies' *Red Deer* on the Golsoncott shelves, as one might expect – exact accounts of Exmoor ecology, red-deer habits and hunting practice.

Henry Williamson also wrote of the Exmoor deer, in 1931, prompted by the bill before Parliament in that year to put forward the pro-hunting argument, much as today's defenders of stag-hunting do. That bill failed; one notes that the arguments on both sides almost precisely parallel those favoured today, with the then League for the Prohibition of Cruel Sports acting as advocates of the bill. Williamson's impassioned defence reads a little oddly, given the theme of *Tarka the Otter*, in which the eponymous hero is hunted to death by the otter hounds. But Williamson was clearly a rum bird, and consistency may not have been high on his agenda. Fervent advocacy of the glories of nature and of wildlife was his signature tune, putting a new spin on the nature novel, but in direct descent from Jefferies and Hudson.

Leslie Stephen was sardonic about nature writing in the *Cornhill Magazine* of 1880: 'Our guide may save us the trouble of stumbling through farmyards and across ploughed fields, but he must have gone through it himself until his very voice has a twang of true country accent.' He was discussing writers such as William Cobbett, Izaak Walton, Gilbert White and George Borrow, but the point applies just as well to later exponents of rural life. Books like these are the armchair experience of the country – precursors of travel writing. And while such literature was indeed produced by countrymen, it was written with an urban readership in mind: vicarious enjoyment, Arcadia without the inconvenience of mud and rain.

But the rural literature cult of the late nineteenth and early twentieth centuries is only a part of it. Earlier, the Romantic poets had set the tone. And before that still the eighteenth-century invention of the picturesque had literally turned landscape into art. If the prospect was not sufficiently pleasing, you tweaked and groomed until it was. Significantly, conspicuous evidence of agricultural activity became undesirable, save for a handful of aesthetically acceptable cattle or a strategically placed cottage. The eighteenth-century landowner under the thrall of Lancelot Brown or Humphrey Repton, arbiters of taste, would sweep away an entire hamlet in the interests of scenic perfection. Those who tilled the fields were to be kept out of sight, and indeed the very fields themselves – the ideal world was a natural one, apparently uncontaminated by human intervention. This preference persists today: most people's model landscape would be a sweep of the Lake District, Exmoor, the Cornish coast or the Scottish Highlands, rather than the farming acreage of East Anglia. Painting of the Constable school may have launched a thousand calendars, but the rustic figures there are adjuncts to a pastoral ideal, a necessary complement to the stream, the tree, the sky. They are points of reference, figures in a landscape like the sylvan intruders of Claude Lorrain.

The pastoral idealism of art and literature reaches back into the distant past, back to Virgil. There is a sense in which the vision has scarcely changed, which is why the *Eclogues* and *Georgics* fall easily on the modern ear. The idea of the country as paradise is centuries deep, a conditioning that has simply been reinforced over time, its assumptions shifting a little here and there, but resolute in its vision of that desirable world which is a convenient mental reconstruction of the real thing.

When children write poetry, they write about nature: rain, snow, fire, ice, my hamster. The invisible directing hand of the teacher is often evident here, as I realized when serving as one of the judges for a national children's writing competition – a slew of poems about pikes, crackling with the influence of Ted Hughes, batches that celebrated rainbows or feathers or the new moon. But there was frequently a verve and a veracity about the writing that was clearly quite independent of any adult's dictation. The physical world is astonishing and unexpected, for every child; it serves up some new surprise each day. As children, we see afresh, we look with an intensity that we will never recover and we look most intensely at nature, at growth and regeneration, at the turning of the world. No wonder, then, that when children find the power of words it is the world around them that prompts the language.

That world is most likely to be an urban one. But it is still infused with potent symbols. I remember a clutch of primary schoolchildren on the pavement alongside the panting traffic of City Road, in London, huddled intently over something at the base of a sickly tree. What were they looking at? A caterpillar. And everyone visits the country, nowadays, or sees it roll past through the windows of a train or car. It is impossible to recover that profound divide, that mutual ignorance before the railway system fingered its way out across the map, and especially before the car achieved absolute authority. The huge expansion in car ownership between the wars – 2 million cars by 1939 – brought the countryside within reach of suburbia, but further down the economic scale it was cycling and hiking that sent unprecedented numbers of people out into the landscape. You put yourself on the train – or yourself and your bike – and there you were, lord of the universe for a day, or a weekend. It is an exodus that has seen exponential growth over the century, but the bikes are mostly gone, and many of the hikers with them; now it is just the cars that glitter from coast to coast – 8 million by 1960, 26 million today, 70 per cent of households on wheels.

This is no place for the pro- and anti-car debate. The point here is simply that transport, over the last hundred years, has brought town and country face to face. There was mutual ignorance still in the first half of the century, which was exposed by the evacuation exercise of the 1940s; since then, the two nations have looked each other in the eye, a process which may have served to distance rather than to unite.

There is something distinctly bizarre about the way in which fox-hunting seems to have become the central issue in the town and country divide, over recent years. Only a very small proportion of the rural population is directly involved in hunting, whether by way of employment or as participants. Many city dwellers would only vaguely be aware of the activity, were they not briskly reminded by the media. But it has become a political matter, an eccentric symbol of difference and dissent.

In the past, the image of hunting was that of archetypal Englishness: picturesque, time-honoured, the expression of an ancient tradition. It was never that, except in the sense that the pursuit of animals is one of the most atavistic practices still around, first recorded in the caves of Lascaux and Altamira, subject matter for art and literature the world over ever since. But fox-hunting is a parvenu where man's engagement with animals is concerned. The primeval incentive for hunting was simply hunger, but there must always have been that element of exhilaration, the rush of adrenalin, the satisfaction at testing skills and experience. Eventually the entertainment aspect of hurtling in pursuit of dinner overtakes the practical to such an extent that the prey must be reserved for the privileged. Medieval hunting was the preserve of the aristocracy. Peasants were strung up for poaching deer. By the nineteenth century errant farmers could be hauled before the magistrates for the crime of vulpicide, the killing of a fox other than by hunting it with hounds. But by then the quarry was inedible, and few countrymen would have stepped out of line anyway: hunting was now subsumed into the structured hierarchy of rural life, shoring up the authority of the landed proprietor, its conventions serving as social reinforcers.

At Golsoncott, the front door opened into the vestibule, a small circular hallway. Its walls were hung with hunting trophies: brushes, deer slots, fox masks – all of them desperately moth-eaten, each with a little plaque recording the date and extent of the run. Down in the stables, the harness room was another shrine to the horse-and-hound culture of the area, decked out with faded rosettes – red, blue, white – recalling past successes at Dunster Show. Firsts and Seconds and Reserves in hunter classes; Commended in the Open Jumping. The achievement of Gaiety Girl, Gay Dream, Roland, Juno and the rest. My aunt kept two horses always, three when the current brood mare had an offspring that would later be sold off. Hunters, all of them – professionals, as it were – whose daily regime dictated the pattern of the day. Exercise, every morning – long leisurely rides in summer, when the horses were out at grass, punishing workouts in the autumn when they were being got into condition for the coming season. I was taken along, on a borrowed pony that couldn't or wouldn't keep up, frantically digging my heels into its sides as Rachel pounded away out of sight. I can smell the harness room to this day: hay and saddle soap and leather and horse. Winter mornings with ice-cold water in a bucket, doing all that post-exercise washing-up of the tack; the elaborate grooming operation of hunting days. But I was a disappointing disciple. Eventually it was tacitly agreed that I was not cut out for serious horse business. By the time I was seventeen, I was allowed to potter around the landscape by myself on an elderly mare equally disinclined for anything at all taxing.

Rachel's combination of interests was esoteric. As a young woman in the 1920s and 1930s she must have been unique – an avant-garde artist who was also a fervent horsewoman, hunting regularly. Her artistic talent was exceptional and her range covered wood engraving, sculpture, painting, the creation of inn signs, and metalwork. She studied art at Iain Macnab's Grosvenor School of Modern Art: wood engraving with Macnab himself, linocutting with Claude Flight and Cyril Power. Her work puts her in the first rank of twentieth-century wood engravers. Her output was considerable – some fine, large wood sculptures during the early period, along with works in stone, often grey and pink alabaster from the coast at Watchet, as well as the more formal limestone, many watercolour and oil paintings – the style and technique changing radically over the years. She was influenced by Cubism and flirted with Surrealism, constantly experimenting, though she always retained the excitement and engagement of those contemporary with the Modern Movement. In her youth, she made the sequence of inn signs that still enliven the area – the Valiant Soldier in Roadwater, the White Horse at Washford, the Butchers Arms at Carhampton and others – several of them early experiments in metalwork. In her last decades, this became her favoured form. She learned how to weld when in her seventies (previously she had been using rivets), branched out with some adventurous compositions and became a revered member of the Artists-Blacksmiths Association (one of the only women at international gatherings amid brawny male practitioners of this highly physical art form). Her metal sculptures are now widely dispersed, but several grace local churches in west Somerset – notably Leighland, Rodhuish and Old Cleeve.

But on hunting days she became someone else. She frequently rode side-saddle and dressed the part, setting aside her usual impatiently dismissive attitude towards clothes and tendency to turn out in anything that came to hand. Hunting was another matter: black habit and hunting coat, spanking-white stock, polished boots, bowler and veil. It was the veil that did it, I seem to remember – she became vaguely mysterious, a Henry James woman, intrepid, handsome and a touch unapproachable. Especially so if mounted on Roland, a half-Arab black stallion of famously capricious behaviour; you kept well clear of Roland, a creature so charged with well-being that he seemed like a coiled spring, barely controllable. He and Rachel were a renowned partnership, crashing a hectic and unstoppable course through the jumps at Dunster Show each summer, to yells of encouragement from the appreciative local crowd.

Those impelled to hunt do so for a diversity of reasons, and ever have. Rachel would have felt at home in the climate of eighteenth-century fox-hunting, when the squirearchy was principally interested in the intricacies of hound work, rather than in the headlong dash across the countryside favoured by feckless young bloods and providing the emphasis of the mid nineteenth-century sport. She hunted for the riding opportunities offered, for the experience of exploring and enjoying the landscape, and for the technical interest of hound skills. Had she come across it, she probably would have seized on Trollope's defence of the sport, which homed in on the point that, unlike such activities as bear- and bull-baiting, cock-fighting or the persecution of animals as an arena spectacle in Roman times, the death of the fox is in a sense a side issue for the hunter. The infliction of cruelty is not the central purpose of hunting; the participant is not therefore degraded in the same way as the spectator at a baiting or a cock-fight. The argument is a dodgy one, but the novelist – an ardent hunting man – had been provoked into a response by the attack upon hunting delivered in the *Fortnightly Review* in 1869 by E. A. Freeman, later Regius Professor of History at Oxford. There had been criticism of hunting over time, but this was the most serious, prominent and carefully thought-out attack yet, arguing that while it is acceptable to kill animals out of need – to eat, or by way of pest control – to inflict cruelty in the service of sport is indefensible. Bull- and bear-baiting and cock-fighting had by then been outlawed, but the debate was still fresh in people's minds, as was the knowledge that some had defended these sports partly because they tacitly recognized that banning traditional recreations of the poor was hardly equitable while hunting, the entertainment of the wealthy, remained immune.

Where the fox was concerned back then, the conservation argument could be put forward – that without the preservation factor of hunting, the species would be exterminated because of its depredations on poultry. Freeman had admitted the validity of this point. But in the early nineteenth century the surging popularity of hunting had resulted in a serious shortage of foxes. The measures taken to remedy this are significant. The most visible and lasting was the effect on the landscape of the wholesale planting by landowners of coverts – small stands of woodland in agricultural country – intended to serve as places for foxes to breed and go to ground. But at some points in the early part of the century fox numbers had fallen so low that it was necessary to resort to desperate devices: the purchase of foxes from areas where they were more prolific, 'bagging' foxes – bringing them in bags and releasing them for the occasion of a hunt – and even – most desperate remedy of all – importing foxes from France. This trade is peculiarly interesting in the xenophobic response that it provoked: French foxes were denounced as effete creatures, the introduction of which would contaminate the bloodline of the stout British fox, a view which meshed with the Francophobia of the age.

The case made for fox-hunting as a means of controlling fox numbers was never very plausible. Before the switch from deer- to fox-hunting in the eighteenth century the fox had been regarded simply as vermin, killed by all countrymen to protect their poultry and to some extent for the use of fox skins. Villages would organize a fox extermination day along the same lines as a rat-hunt. But the early nineteenth-century shortage made it clear that in fact conservation measures were now necessary, along with some way of ensuring that all surviving foxes were reserved for the purposes of hunting – hence the invocation of vulpicide. The fox was still vermin, but vermin with a special status.

The fox has had a bad image. In practical terms, it was the ravager of farmyard poultry, but alongside that was its literary persona – cunning, ruthless and unreliable, a stock character of folklore and fairy tale, its role as a villain wrapped up conclusively by Beatrix Potter with Mr Todd. Deer, on the other hand, were seen as noble creatures, the stag as the last word in majesty and courage. Think of *Monarch of the Glen*. The chroniclers of Exmoor stag-hunting write with rapture and respect of the lifestyle of the red deer, while the fox is only of circumstantial interest to fox-hunting experts on account of its strategies for outwitting a pack of hounds. Perhaps all this is coloured by the question of edibility, and there have always been those whose perception of deer was rather different – notably medieval peasants who had to put up with their crops being eaten by the sacred quarry of the nobility.

Deer have been the favoured prey all over Europe since antiquity: reasonably abundant, excellent eating. The fore-runners of *Monarch of the Glen* are those murky shapes on the walls of Lascaux. But with the erosion of forests and woodland through the Middle Ages deer numbers fell dramatically – hence the draconian game laws of the period. Hunting was limited strictly to the upper classes – the sport of kings in France, and indeed in this country too, though by the seventeenth century in England deer parks owned by country gentle-men were widespread, the source not only of sport but also of fresh meat. Private packs of hounds had long been around, the creatures ancestral to the hound of today. Hound-breeding became a central concern; the aesthetics of hunting required a choice cry as well as good pace, hounds being selected for bass, tenor and counter-tenor, with beagles supplying the treble. Hares were also seen as acceptable quarry, but the hare does not run in a straight line – at some point in the eighteenth century hunting squires began to discover the virtues of the fox when it came to a stimulating run across country. Deer were becoming even more scarce, but foxes, at that point, were abundant. The apparently traditional sport of fox-hunting was born, something over a couple of hundred years ago, launching a blizzard of sporting prints and creating an imper-ishable image of rural life.

The eighteenth-century fox-hunting squire had been a con-noisseur of hounds and their skills, above all. By the mid nineteenth century there had been a radical change in both the style and significance of fox-hunting. As its popularity grew, not only for the participants but as a spectator sport for country people who turned out to see the nobs go by, so its status changed from a private to a public activity. The subscription pack took the place of the local squire's privately owned pack. This was the age of the country house, the apex of the rural social hierarchy; hunting as an activity was now integrated into the social system and the hunting field became an arena for advancement in society.

The nineteenth-century hunting gentleman liked to charge his way across the countryside as fast as possible and for as long as possible. The more jumps available, the better. It was during this period that a hierarchy of packs developed, with the Midlands emerging as the prime hunting country on account of its enclosure landscape with plenty of hedges to provide excitement and abundant grassland for the good hard gallop. Another factor was the railway system. The city-based enthusiast could now hunt from London, travelling in a first-class carriage with his horses and groom in a rail horsebox. Trollope used to do this – a day's hunting in Leicestershire and back to town by evening. His vision of the rural landscape, indeed, seems to have been as a convenient backdrop for fox-hunting, given that 'the owner of the land, with all the law to back him, with his right to the soil as perfect and as exclusive as that of a lady to her drawing-room, cannot in effect save himself from an invasion of a hundred or a hundred and fifty horsemen, let him struggle to save himself as he may.' But few would be inclined to struggle: 'It may be said that in a real hunting county active antagonism to hunting is out of the question. A man who cannot endure to see a crowd of horse-men on his land, must give up his land and go elsewhere to live.'

Quite so. Hunting by that point was a crucial part of the social fabric. You could just about get away with not riding to hounds yourself and retain social credibility, but any demon-stration of disapproval would have been unthinkable, and for the socially aspirant it was expedient to cut a dash on the hunting field. A situation that no doubt continues to this day, in some quarters, and certainly did in west Somerset in the late 1940s. I had not read Jane Austen by then and so could not appreciate the resonances in the situation of a neighbour, a genteel lady in reduced circumstances, possessed of two fine daughters in their late teens, neither of them qualified in any way either for employment or for higher education. Early marriage was imperative. There was nothing for it but to get them on horseback and in the hunting field where they could best be displayed to the eligible bachelors of the area. The spa and the ballroom being no longer much around, this was the most practical substitute. The wretched girls, who disliked riding, spent a miserable season smiling bravely in the rain and the wind and doing their best to avoid having to take any jumps or proceed at more than a cautious trot. Their mother's strategy paid off and both achieved what in Austen terms would be seen as highly satisfactory alliances – the local pack had served its purpose as social catalyst.

Those for whom fox-hunting was an accustomed element of rural life had neither time nor taste for the moral debate. But the rise of hunting in the eighteenth century took place against a changing climate of enlightened opinion about the treatment of animals. The casual cruelty of early periods stemmed essentially from a perception of animals as being of a different order and thus not susceptible to suffering in the same way as people. It was the cruelty of indifference, rather than that of the witting infliction of pain. The sight of an animal in distress did not affect the onlooker. Indeed, the early arguments against activities which involved cruelty to animals focused not upon the feelings of the animal but upon the corrupting effect on the person involved – those accustomed to tormenting animals might go on to do the same to fellow humans. But by the eighteenth century there was growing support for the idea that the unnecessary infliction of suffering on animals should be avoided on purely humanitarian grounds – it was wrong because the animal suffered, regardless of the implications for any people involved. Such convictions paved the way for the establishment of the Society for the Prevention of Cruelty to Animals in 1824 and the passage of various Acts of Parliament in the early part of the century against cruelty to horses, cattle and dogs and the abolition of baiting and cock-fighting.

Hunting, shooting and fishing now stood alone, as they still do, the last two bolstered against criticism by their association with legitimate slaughter in pursuit of a meal. Hunting was always more problematic, involving as it did the element of class interest along with such factors as the inedibility of foxes and the perceived charm of deer and hares. The arguments both for its defence and its abolition got caught up in issues subsidiary to the central debate over whether or not it is cruel to hunt an animal with dogs. Today, the activity has somehow achieved its current anachronistic role as the focus of disagreement between town and country.

England in 1945 bewildered me, a refugee in this place that was apparently the homeland. Its most perplexing aspects were these appositions: the confusing contrasts of class, with codes that I could not appreciate, the opposing worlds of town and country. London and west Somerset seemed hardly to occupy the same planet, and felt much that way about one another. Egypt had been a place of violent contrasts, a cultural cauldron, polyglot and cosmopolitan, but its discords were unstructured, disorganized and unpredictable. In England it was clear that there was structure, there was a system and there were complex arrangements of mutual exclusion. By far the most baffling and treacherous was that of social hierarchy, but the town-and-country thing ran it a close second. Fifty years later, the divide remains, but is now blurred by familiarity and by universal mobility. The two nations know all about each other, or think that they do, and certainly quite enough to foster argument and misunderstanding.

When I used to go by train to Somerset from London for the school holidays, each compartment held framed photographs of selected glories of the West Country: Land's End, Dunkery Beacon, Clovelly, Tintagel. You knew that you were going to another place. At Taunton I changed on to the branch line to Minehead, replicating the journey made by my grandmother and her siblings in the 1890s. The city fell away as I stepped onto that second train; now the country had taken over, with all that implied – different voices, different assumptions, another set of values. By the time I reached Washford station, London was not just a couple of hundred miles away, but a world apart. I had crossed a frontier. Today, I still make that journey, a Great Western train is still following Brunel's foray west. But the train journey ends at Taunton, and its climate is very different. People do not cross a frontier, but merely slip from one environment to another. There are those who live down west but work in London, their lives expanded by new technology. A fellow passenger tells me that he spends his weekends at home in a village near Exeter and commutes up to town for the week, where he works as an executive limousine chauffeur. The rise of the Quantocks on the skyline still announces that we are nearly there, but there is no longer that tacit ritual of departure and arrival.

The Dressing-Room, the Nursery and the Grand Piano

For a dozen years, until I was married, my room at Golson-cott was the one then still known as the dressing-room. My grandfather's dressing-room. Next door to my grandmother's large bedroom, it overlooked the canal garden, the windows wreathed in wisteria. The bed had a horsehair mattress, considered healthy and desirable in the 1920s and '30s; I thought its unrelenting hardness normal and acceptable until I came across springs. I imagine that the bed had been his. Whether or not he and my grandmother shared her bedroom I do not know, but the very existence of the dressing-room, integral to domestic arrangements, is an indication of the gulf in assumptions about marriage and about the place of men and women then and now. Maybe there are still households in which a dressing-room is taken for granted, but, for me, it has become an interesting symbol of change and contrast.

I know that my marriage was qualitatively different from my grandmother's. Not in the obvious sense that every marriage is a unique transaction, but in its expectations and its practices, which were dictated by the times, in both cases. My grandmother's was also a long marriage, curtailed only by death, but it was without the intimacy, the edge, the eyeball-to-eyeball quality of late twentieth-century marriage. My grandparents gave each other space, in the phraseology of a later age, but that was owed more to the fact that they occupied different spaces. In one sense this was literal – that dressing-room, my grandfather's sacrosanct study in which he spent much of the day – but it was a division that was concerned also with hard-and-fast rules about who did what around the place. My grandmother supervised domestic matters and ruled supreme in the garden; my grandfather's involvement was with the upkeep and running of the stables. He had trained as an architect but seems not to have practised for long and by the time the family moved to Somerset he was in retirement, his main occupation riding and hunting. I never really knew him. He died in 1941, and my only memory slide in which he features is one from the summer before the war. I am on the veranda. I feel something on my leg and look down: there on my calf is a black slug. I shriek. The adults admonish in dismay. And sure enough, my grandfather emerges from his study, *The Times* in one hand, looking like thunder. I am whisked away, still keening about the slug. Grandchildren should be seen but not heard.

Looking back – making comparisons – the gender divide in the first half of the century seems not a distinction but a chasm. My grandmother's late Victorian youth was typical of her class and set an inexorable pattern – boys were raised entirely by women in the nursery but then packed off to boarding school and the company solely of other males. Girls stayed at home, for the most part. From then on the gulf was bridged formally only by marriage; the unspoken assumption was that men and women were profoundly different in their needs, tastes, attitudes. And up to a point this is of course true, but it has long since ceased to be institutionalized in quite that way, except in the arcane worlds of men's clubs or on the foot-ball terraces. In 1950 I was aware of a potent whiff of these beliefs at Golsoncott where, without my grandfather, things had settled to a comfortably female-oriented household. Male visitors caused a flurry of disquiet: could the domestic arrangements rise to the occasion? A man would expect a cooked breakfast (not on offer to women guests). He would need his shoes cleaned and must be supplied with alcohol and cigarettes.

My grandmother – a forceful and strong-minded woman – saw men simply as another species. Their inclinations and appetites were not those of women, their capacities were other and I think, by implication, superior. Financial matters were best left to men. Women of her kind chose to remain in considerable ignorance of their economic circumstances, as though it were in some way unbecoming to cast a sharp eye over the accounts – a stance only possible, of course, for the affluent, but surely an uncomfortable legacy of the financial status of the Victorian wife or daughter.

Trying to think my way into her perception of the gender divide it seems to me to have been based on a profound lack of intimacy with men, which itself stemmed from deep social assumptions about the respective roles of men and women. Her own marriage was not a close one; her Victorian father would have been a distant figure. Those turn-of-the-century photographs of Exmoor summer gatherings propose a jolly family of siblings, but even there the apartness sneaks out: my grandmother and her sister always together, the brothers as that uniformed brigade – the Men. And if women saw men as *sui generis*, the view must have been equivalent from the other side. There is a kind of defiant nervousness about my uncles' versifying, when it comes to a vision of women, which meshes with more sophisticated literary attitudes. A confused mixture of gallantry, protectiveness, patronage, incomprehension and alarm.

My uncles were unusual in their bachelordom. Marriage was the norm. Pairing off and procreation – the rituals of all time and every place. The photograph albums in the hall chest recorded many family weddings in the twenties and thirties; the brides looking very young and flanked by a line of grown-up bridesmaids, whose turn would come next, mothers and aunts done up in fox furs and adventurous hats, the men in ceremonial tailcoats. There is an atmosphere of occasion, of formality, but also of completion. There stand bride and groom, prinked, polished and presented to the camera with complacent pride. What ought to be done has been done.

My aunt Rachel sometimes featured in the bridesmaid line-ups, tricked out in ankle-length satin, a wreath on her head, clutching a posy and wearing an expression of rebellious resignation. She would have hated the whole business. Dressing-up was anathema to her, and large-scale events something of an ordeal. She was energetic and independent, but also oddly shy and diffident, as well as impatient with the ritual exchanges of social life. She needed to be in her studio working, or out there with horse and dogs in the hills and on the moor. She never married. I cannot think that this was for lack of suitors. She is appealingly pretty in those early photos, but the soft English-rose looks were deceptive. Rachel was briskly unconventional beneath the veneer of her circumstances. Perhaps the suitors sensed this; perhaps she herself had some instinctive urge towards solitude. She was intensely involved in her work, always experimenting, switching to some new medium or method. And as she moved through the century she became interestingly in tune with it. When she was a young woman, that pejorative word spinster was still around, and must have hung about her, unspoken. By the time she was in her seventies, still richly creative, the very concept was extinguished. As one of the few women working with metal as an artist-blacksmith, she became something of a feminist icon, which both amused and pleased her. And she flourished in a more flexible and expansive social climate. On her own patch, down there in west Somerset, she was a hallowed figure, known far and wide, still bucketing through the lanes in a beat-up old Land-Rover when in her eighties.

One weekend in 1956 I visited my father in London. I was then living and working in Oxford. On the Sunday evening he drove me to Paddington to catch the train back. He was rather silent, as though something were on his mind. As we waited at a traffic light on Kensington Gore (I know which one, to this day), he spoke, abruptly: 'There's something I've been meaning to say to you. Isn't it about time you were thinking of getting married?'

I was twenty-three. I had a job, so was financially independent. I remember being startled – this seemed an injunction from another time. I would have thought it more appropriate if he had been concerned about my career prospects, which were not sparkling in view of my somewhat dead-end occupation. I think I protested that I had nobody in mind at that moment, nor did it seem that anybody had me in mind. The subject was dropped, and as it happened someone did hove on the scene very shortly. I was married within the year, so my father had no need to pursue the matter. I sometimes wonder how he would have proceeded if things had not turned out thus.

My father was also, I think, conditioned by the assumptions of an earlier age. Perhaps we all are, by the time we get to middle life – still jumping to the tune of our own salad days. He saw marriage as an essential rite of passage for a young woman. His sisters had been married in their early twenties; it was his paternal duty to make some cautionary noises.

And I would not have been entirely unresponsive. My

childhood was not so distant, with its own tenacious subliminal conditioning. A concept of marriage was central to that conditioning. It was a concept derived quite as much from literature as from observation. I grew up surrounded by the married friends of my parents, and at a time when divorce was unusual, but my vision of marriage was not so much that of real life as the one fostered by childhood reading. Marriage as a goal and culmination. Marriage as in fairy stories: 'And so they were married and lived happily ever after.' Marriage as the essential arrival at maturity, for girls above all. Moreover, this mythology permeated nursery rituals. I was growing up in the expatriate British community in Cairo before and during the war, a society in which mothers on the whole did not look after their own children. I was cared for by Lucy, a figure far more central to me than my own mother. Our joint social life consisted of teatime get-togethers with other families. At such gatherings Lucy and her fellow nannies would conduct fortune-telling sessions with the tea leaves left in their cups. A twig-like fragment was a tall dark stranger; a circular arrangement was a wedding ring. There was competition for the last sandwich on the plate, which allowed for a choice between a handsome husband or 10,000 a year. No one ever opted for the 10,000. If I stuck my tongue out or pulled faces, Lucy would tell me crisply that the wind would change and I'd be stuck like that, 'and then nobody will want to marry you'. The fact that she herself was unmarried remained unspoken.

There was a programme, it seemed, and marriage was its crucial and central plank. Marriage was an end in itself, and you did not look beyond it. There would be children, of course, which were inevitable, unimaginable and not particularly interesting. Sex hardly came into it. I was passionately addicted to Greek mythology as a child, which was full of pairings and alliances – not always straight marriages, making them a touch confusing – and the erotic overtones seeped through to me, but not in any specific way, simply as some elusive atmospheric that lent spice and flavour.

Marriage was the essential goal, apparently, and the implication was that it was permanent. Divorce was, of course, around but it was uncommon and uneasy – a shifty word, mentioned only in an undertone. I had heard it, just, but as one of those mysterious adult references, which one must not pursue. Something dark and not quite nice. Later, after my parents' divorce, when my mother had remarried and dropped out of my life for a couple of years and I was living with my father, it homed in with a vengeance. I was now branded myself – a child of divorce, which was not a good thing to be, and I must not refer to the matter unless absolutely necessary. Grown-ups would murmur amongst themselves and eye me sympathetically. The sympathy made me feel important but the status was clearly undesirable.

Very different fifty years later, thanks be. Divorce remains a grim experience for all concerned, but the many children affected no longer feel unique, stigmatized, in some puzzling way disreputable. They will all know others in the same position. The word itself is defused. It has implications, but is no longer loaded, no longer carries a freight of unmentionable things. A status now, and that is that. Equally, the single parent is simply a social category. My father, single-parenting in the late 1940s, was an object of pity and a certain prurient interest. Fashionable women friends took me shopping for clothes and came back with garments he considered unsuitable and too expensive. More crucially, he had to cope with a difficult adolescent traumatized by the combination of family break-up and removal from the childhood home in Egypt to this chill and alien place, England. No solicitous counselling available back then. The ethos of the times was that, in the face of misfortune, you buckled to and got on with things. And if the misfortune was divorce, the less said the better.

Jack and I opted for a register office wedding. We were both agnostic, in any case, but also disliked the pomp and circumstance of a religious ceremony, and the faintly threatening overtones of the script: 'For better, for worse, till death us do part.' We hoped and assumed that we would stay married, but did not want the magisterial intervention of organized religion. Kensington Register Office was depressing and mundane. We sat in awkward silence in a dark-brown waiting-room, with the two friends brought along as witnesses; at one point a functionary put his head round the door and said sternly: 'Would you mind making less noise?' At that moment, I thought a little wistfully of organ music and dear little bridesmaids. But the reception later that day was plumb in the traditional marriage mode, with the stock assemblage of ill-assorted relatives and attendant cast of friends of bride and groom who do not know one another – a curious set-piece occasion that takes place worldwide and throughout the years because two people have met and bring with them their respective freight of others. We escaped to a honeymoon in Brittany and the beginning of a different life.

A commencement, of course, rather than the culmination suggested by all that misleading childhood reading. The setting forth into a future in which 'I' had become 'we', in which to be alone was to be just the two of you, in which opinions, decisions, moods, every swing and roundabout of life would be shared with someone else, from now on into incalculable distances of time. Forty-one years, as it turned out. Until the autumn night on which I would walk out of a north London hospice, alone once more. But not entirely, because there were now those whose infinitely familiar presences were unimaginable back then: our children, and theirs.

Every marriage is a journey, a negotiation, an accommodation. In a long marriage, both partners will mutate; the people who set out together are not the same two people after ten years, let alone thirty or more. When accommodation is no longer possible it is usually because one or the other has become so much someone else as to be unreachable. Our marriage was like most; it had its calm reaches, its sudden treacherous bends, its episodes of white water to be navigated with caution and a steady nerve. We were poles apart temperamentally. Jack was volatile, confrontational, a natural radical, a man who relished intellectual debate; he was also loving and generous. I was – am, I suppose – more equable, less disputatious, and without his incisive mind. That said, we meshed entirely in tastes and inclinations, could always fire one another with a new interest, and laid down over the years that rich sediment of shared references and mutual recognition familiar to all who have known a long companionship. You are separate people, but there is a third shadowy presence which is an entity, the fusion of you both. It is your corporate experience – a private existence invisible and impenetrable to others. When this is extinguished, you are left with only the ambivalent solace of having once known that mysterious and miraculous creation of shared lives.

Marriage is the most contingent event of any. We marry – or pair off with – the person who appears when the time is ripe, when mood and circumstance coincide with a significant encounter. When we meet the right person at the right time. Had the coin fallen differently – had we not gone to that particular gathering, taken that job, got talking to that stranger

– the rest of life would have spun off in other directions. The solid reality of our children would not have been. It is a perennially unsteadying thought that we owe our existence to the fortuitous conjunction of our parents, who might never have come across one another. The marriage scenario is the ultimate garden of forked paths.

Anyone spending the crucial years of their early twenties in an academic setting, as I did, is spoiled for choice, when it comes to pairing off arrangements. St Antony's College in Oxford, where I met Jack, was – and is – a graduate college, cosmopolitan and – back then – a relatively small enclave of diverse and vibrant people. All male, in the 1950s. I was not a member of the college but working as research assistant to one of the fellows. This meant, though, that I was in the thick of college life, which in turn rippled off into the wider world of the university. Abundant opportunities to meet young men: parties, seminars, the libraries in which I researched for my employer. I had an office in one of the college houses in Woodstock Road. Members of the college were in and out of its front door all day, Israeli, American, French, German; there were coffee breaks, sandwich lunches. I stepped out for a while with a wild Welshman and spent summer evenings driving to Oxfordshire pubs with him and John Bayley, who was then at St Antony's, in an old Riley (with running boards), belonging to Iris Murdoch, whom John was courting. It was a heady time, and seems in retrospect to have gone on for years, but in fact lasted barely two. I remember hearing one of the fellows talking about the new Junior Research Fellow coming from Cambridge the following term: 'Jack Lively – extremely bright'. The name stuck in my mind – I thought he sounded like a character in an eighteenth-century novel. Less than a year later we were married.

This degree of opportunity for choice is a privilege, and one unknown to many young people across time and space. The skirmishing of matchmaking mothers is the stuff of nineteenth-century literature, trying to marry off daughters in pinched social circumstances. Rural life has ever been hard on romance. In west Somerset in the 1950s, it would have been rare for a young man or woman to marry anyone from beyond a radius of five miles or so. A local doctor used to say that he could tell from which Exmoor village a person came by the shape of their heads. In the more distant past, rural inbreeding must have been rampant. And under some conditions choice becomes so narrowed down that contingency barely plays a part. The line-up of those available is so short as to serve up nothing but an inevitability. Looked at in this light, marriage seems more like a grim social and biological necessity than the enriching rite of passage celebrated in fairy tale and mythology. A necessity and, in some instances, a prison.

And now, at the beginning of a new century, marriage in this country seems to be a precarious institution. In the sense not only that over one in three fail, but also that it is now merely an option. And this has as much to do with changed perceptions of gender as with an altered view of the arrangement itself. Something happened around the middle of the century, some incipient awakening which meant that a twenty-three-year-old girl was surprised to be told by her father that she should be thinking of getting married.

Feminism happened, of course, but it hadn't happened by 1956. We hadn't heard of role-playing back then, and gender had more to do with Latin nouns than negotiations between men and women. My own experience of the opposite sex was circumscribed, to say the least. I had been at a girls' boarding school, and when I arrived at Oxford at eighteen, I had never spoken to a boy of my own age. And now here was a sea of them, done up identically in grey flannels and duffel coats, ten to every one of us girls. A culture shock – though the difficulties evaporated after a week or two and were a distant memory by the end of the first term.

Oxford in the 1950s seems a world away from student life fifty years later. That gender imbalance, the segregation of men and women, with its elaborate rules designed to maintain the distance and thus, I suppose, reduce sexual opportunity. Sex being, of course, as rampant as you might expect – but we made less fuss about it. In my college, there was an 11.15 p.m. curfew – back in by then, or see the Principal next morning and explain why not – and a period of licence between two and seven in the afternoon when you might receive male visitors. Tea and crumpets. Et cetera. The assumption made by the college authorities seems to have been that sex would rear its ugly head only after dark; out with temptation at 7 p.m. and all would be well. We went along with this, there being little choice, and the more daring made their own arrangements. One girl in my hostel regularly had her boyfriend to stay overnight, smuggling him out through the window in the morning. The rest of us were well aware of his presence and said nowt, though those in adjoining rooms were irritated by the squeaking of the bed. We did not much discuss our sexual experiences, not, I think, out of discretion but because the whole issue was tainted by fear: in those pre-Pill days grim tales of clandestine abortion haunted us all. There was much scared and private counting of days and watching of the calendar. Each of us knew or knew of some girl to whom it had actually happened: that awful realization, the nausea, the panic.

This was no climate of sexual liberation – it is strange now to think that the sixties were only ten years off. But it was a climate of new expectations and assumptions for women graduates. Towards the end of the third year, students were supposed to go for an interview at the University Appointments Board. You offered your qualifications, such as they were, and stated your preferences for future employment. Women arts undergraduates were overwhelmingly enthusiastic about the B B C and publishing. Those heading for a First considered the Civil Service exam. But many were happy to go into teaching, then still a respected and valued profession. The steely eyed staff of the Appointments Board were keen to steer women into the relatively untried areas of industry and commerce, which alarmed most of us because you had to have shorthand and typing, which meant a slog at some secretarial school. Note that this would never have been required of male applicants for similar jobs. We did take note, and were properly indignant – and suspicious of what roles we would be playing if we fell for this discrimination.

But the Appointments Board was, by and large, on our side, and its attitudes were certainly in line with the shape of things to come. One unwary friend of mine confided cheerily to her interviewer that she wanted a job for only a year or so – something interesting that would maybe take her abroad – because after that she planned to marry. She was sent off with a flea in her ear. Why take up an expensive and privileged educational opportunity if that is the height of your ambition?

Neither my mother nor my grandmother ever earned a penny. Their lives were based on entirely different assumptions – and resources – from my own, or my daughter's. Or, indeed, those of my granddaughters, who announce crisp and provocative career intentions at an early age. Oh yes, they will be having children, they say, but alongside that they will be astronauts, astronomers, tornado-chasers. My own vision of the future at their age would have been dominated by that hazy but essential state of marriage; it was not until I was eighteen or so that I acquired the sharpened gaze of the mid century and began to focus on other things. Though on quite what I did not know. For the interviewers of the Appointments Board, I would have been one of their many taxing clients with vague aspirations but no clear sense of direction. As it turned out, I was ambushed early by marriage and maternity. I spent five years looking after children and reading my way through the local public library during every available moment. By the time the youngest child went to primary school, I knew that I wanted somehow to use the ideas and enthusiasms prompted by all this serendipitous reading. I seemed to fall into writing almost by accident, though I see now that the urge had probably always been there. My childhood was spent in a state of continuous internal story-telling. All that reading simply fired the mind.

My generation of middle-class women juggled work and childcare. For subsequent generations this is the norm; for ours it was something of a departure, and fuelled a complex mixture of satisfaction and guilt. The satisfactions were evident – you were refusing to be just an appendage, a wife and mother, and doing what any self-respecting late twentieth-century woman should be doing. The guilt – as rife now as then, I suspect – sprang from the evident impossibility of both having a job and being a textbook mother, the texts in our case being the teachings of John Bowlby and Benjamin Spock, the childcare gurus of the day.

Jack's first permanent academic post was at the University of Swansea. A week or so into the first term, we were bidden to a reception given by the Vice Chancellor to kick off the new academic year. As the faculty and spouses (almost exclusively wives – there were few women faculty members) lined up to enter the room, identifying badges were handed out, on which were inscribed name and department. The colour of the badge indicated rank. Thus, my green badge saying 'LIVELY MRS, POLITICS' indicated that I was (Mrs) Lecturer in Politics. I remember that there was a tendency for the women to gather in small groups, eyeing their fellow appendages – (Mrs) Reader in Chemical Engineering or (Mrs) Assistant Lecturer in Sociology. With shared irritation, I hope; certainly I remember feeling affronted.

I had never heard of genetic drive when I was young. But I knew that I would want children, in due course. At some point. In the event, our daughter arrived before I was twenty-five. My generation bred younger than middle-class women of today, who mostly seem to pitch into their thirties before taking that enormous step. We didn't have the Pill, of course, which accounts for much, but also, I think, we were conditioned by the beliefs of the day, which were still much like my father's views – a girl should be married before it began to look odd that she wasn't, and, once married, she should get on with it and have a baby because that was what was expected of her.

At Golsoncott, visiting grandchildren were hived off into the kitchen wing of the house, where were the nursery and night nursery. This arrangement would have reflected that in my grandmother's previous home, where she brought up her own children, an apartheid that symbolizes the difference between Edwardian family life and that of the late twentieth century. It supposes a large house, of course, and plenty of villas and terraced houses up and down the land would not have had the space to function quite like that; nevertheless, the middle-class infrastructure of nursemaids and helpers would have ensured that offspring could be kept apart when required. Children were a crucial aspect of family life, but not the central pivot, which conventionally would have been the father and breadwinner. My grandmother remembered being allowed with her siblings to visit the dining-room on Sunday mornings, where her father was eating his boiled egg, a luxury not issued to the five of them; they took it in turns to have the slice off the top.

All this seems very odd from the viewpoint of the family of the second half of the century, in which the requirements of children dominate household management, and there can be few homes with such a thing as a child-free zone. It seemed odd to me, in the 1950s and '60s, contrasting the manner in which my mother and grandmother had brought up children with the hands-on, no-respite way in which Jack and I were raising ours. I felt a degree of complacent superiority, knowing that we were doing it how it should be done (never mind that there was no alternative) – received opinion of the day was with us to the hilt. On days of unremitting mayhem, and after a night not so much broken as annihilated, the superiority was tinged with furtive envy. My grandmother, who was equally certain that her ways – or the ways of her time – were best, looked on with a sort of resigned perplexity. She couldn't see how I would manage, and the children would undoubtedly suffer.

My mother had operated along the same lines as my grandmother. I grew up apart from my parents, on the whole, in a happy and self-sufficient nursery enclave with Lucy. The effect of this, of course, was that I loved and relied upon Lucy to the exclusion of my parents, with all that that implies. When I had children of my own, I knew that I did not want a repetition of this, but in any case by then the climate was very different. Once again, something had happened in the mid century.

Crucially, my generation could not afford domestic help. But there was more to it than that. Of all dogmas, childcare ones are, perhaps, the most mutable. Strap the baby to a board and hang it on a convenient beam, farm it out to a wet-nurse in some insanitary cottage. Deprive it of fruit and vegetables because these are bad for the digestive system – the ensuing scurvy is attributed to teething problems. Dunk it in an ice-cold bath every day in the interests of healthy development. Some earlier methods of child-rearing sound today more like child abuse. By the twentieth century those involved in childcare, the mother above all, were bombarded with advice and exhortations from successive authorities on the subject. In the early part of the century, Truby King and the Mothercraft movement dominated. Lucy had a copy of the Truby King manual – I can see its blue cover to this day, battered and stained, so evidently much consulted. The Truby King baby was fed by the clock, four-hourly and no night feeds. In between it was exposed to as much fresh air as possible, even spending nights on a veranda or porch. Those infants tactless enough to object to this regime must be left, gently but firmly, to 'cry it out'. The emphasis was on a careful and rigorous training which would produce a biddable and well-behaved child. Manners were high on the agenda and the criterion whereby any child was judged by those in the business: 'Quite a nice little girl,' Lucy would say of some new acquaintance, 'but not good manners, I'm afraid.' Each mealtime was a ritual of saying 'please' and 'thank you', finishing up what was on your plate, and not interrupting or fidgeting.

By the 1950s, Truby King was a dead duck, though that obsession with fresh air somehow lingered on. I can remember dutifully parking the baby in a pram in the garden in midwinter. But our mentor was Benjamin Spock. A paperback copy of his *Common Sense Book of Baby and Child Care* was on every thinking mother's shelf, bringing new ideas and reassurance from across the Atlantic. Small children could indeed be pesky and intransigent, you were told. Babies do not lie docile in their cots between feeds; toddlers have temper tantrums. And it isn't necessarily all your fault: look, try this and see if it works. And this, and this. The index briskly targeted areas of concern. You looked up 'Crying', and worked down the list of possible reasons, from hunger to an open nappy pin. And even if all strategies had failed, you were still told to have faith in yourself and not despair. If your toddler adamantly resisted toilet training, you were to bear in mind that one does not see many adolescents walking around in nappies. The compliant and passive child of the Truby King area had been replaced by a demanding little individual, who might well be fractious and bewildering, but was also responsive and stimulating. Intelligence was riding high now and I don't remember that the inculcation of good manners was much more than a footnote. Which was just as well; the mid century mother had little time left for such refinements, most of us without the benefit of washing-machines or disposable nappies and anxiously focused upon creative play and early learning.

And then there was Bowlby. It is perhaps significant that my copy of the Spock handbook has long since disappeared, ripped up maybe by a creatively playing child, but John Bowlby's Pelican (3s. 6d., first published 1953) is still with me. *Child Care and the Growth of Love* was not a manual but a sombre discussion of the effects on children of maternal deprivation, aimed mainly at social workers and those professionally concerned, but also widely read by mothers in search of up-to-date enlightenment, and it struck fear into the heart. A warm, continuous relationship with the mother throughout its early years was essential to a child's mental health, one was told. A 'mother-substitute' was grudgingly allowed, but she too must be permanent and reliable – no transient carers or fly-by-night au pair girls, by implication. Leaving any child under three, even for a short period, was a major operation only to be undertaken for good and sufficient reason. The mother who had been thinking of slipping off into a job thought again, more responsibly. And those of us already committed to 24-hour, 365-day childcare suffered appalling guilt if we sloped off for a unencumbered shopping expedition or a blissful hour in the library. Fathers were shunted to one side, though granted a certain use in infancy – 'as the illegitimate child knows'. Their prime role was 'to provide for their wives to enable them to devote themselves unrestrictedly to the care of the infant and toddler'. He was there as an economic and emotional support.

Bowlby's dire histories of children traumatized by maternal deprivation were, of course, all drawn from institutionalized cases. But his warnings of the social effects of child neglect – the 'social succession', whereby the neglected child grows up to become the neglectful parent – certainly ring true fifty years later. One valuable result of his influence was a revolution in attitudes towards hospitalized children – the realization by the medical world that children get better sooner if their parents are with them as much as possible rather than if visiting hours are rigidly restricted, as had been the practice. But the average mother of the well-tended child took his admonitions personally and was accordingly caught in a double bind. If you succumbed to the temptations of employment you risked damaging your child's psyche and creating a social psychopath;

if you festered at home in the face of your inclinations and abilities you compromised your own future.

The perception of childhood has undergone a metamorphosis. When I look at photographs of my own parents as children, I see them as a different kind of being from my own young, or the children of today. They are subsumed into the culture of another world – differently treated, differently understood. One day in 1911, my grandmother summoned a studio photographer to take a series of family portraits at her home. The family is posed in various different combinations on a wide chintz-covered window seat: my grandparents, my mother, aged nine, her brother Basil, a few years younger, and Rachel, the baby, about two. My grandfather wears a formal suit, my grandmother is tight-waisted and high-necked, the children are sashed and pin-tucked and knickerbockered. They are beautiful photographs – technically impressive products of the wide-angled lens of the time, dreamily elegant in the arrangement of adults with children, children on their own. All the children have bare feet. Not, I think, to save the chintz covers of the window seat, but in line with a curious fetish of the day.

Another set of photos comes from the other side of my family. My paternal grandmother was a keen amateur photographer, and a very good one too. Her six offspring were her favourite subjects. There they are, in rich sepia, on a Cornish beach, at the same period. The children, ranging from three to about twelve, are stark naked. They have been carefully posed against effective backgrounds, the goose pimples almost palpable, an occasional edge of white protruding beneath them indicating the concession of a towel as padding against the rocks. Photographs such as these would today have high-street photo-developers reaching for the police, in line with one of the twentieth century's most curious inversions, whereby sexual inhibitions are largely non-existent, but the nudity of children can arouse consternation in some quarters. A hundred years ago, a naked child was considered charming. Obviously, there must have been a perverse sexual fascination for a perennial minority, but these implications would not have occurred to the vast majority of people, certainly not to that enthusiastic amateur photographer in 1910 or thereabouts, displaying her brood to best advantage in a Cornish cove. I have always suspected that the insinuations about Lewis Carroll's interest in photographing semi-nude children are entirely misplaced.

Lewis Carroll's insight into the nature of childhood and a child's perception remains unique. *Alice in Wonderland* has been variously interpreted down the years – as a philosophical game, as linguistic play and challenge, as a gloss on Victorian beliefs, as a coded skit on the figures and fashions of the day. Its fantasies have been sternly and soberly re-assessed in the light of other times and allocated appropriate sexual symbolisms: that rabbit hole with its lubricating pots of marmalade, all that growing and shrinking, the phallicism of Alice's elongated neck. Some of the wilder shores of *Alice* criticism make for entertaining reading, and the scholarly decoding of the nonsense verse and of many teasing textual references is endlessly absorbing, but for me the great revelation of this extraordinary work is its skewed world in which the beady eye cast upon anarchy is that of a child, as is the sceptical questioning of apparent irrationality. The blizzard of baffling and confusing instructions and information that falls upon every child everywhere assumes a Carrollian texture.

A fine instance of a book illuminating real life. Read *Alice* in this way and children take on a new significance. But *Alice* has not always been understood thus. In the early part of the century Carroll was stock reading – most middle-class homes would have had his work on the bookshelf – but appreciation focused on the humour, the fantasy world, the Tenniel illustrations. The time was not ripe for a radical view of childhood. In the literature of the day – both for and about children – childhood is a golden age, a happy dreaming time set apart from the rest of life, essentially different because children are indeed different from our adult selves. They are a privileged sect, temporarily occupying this cherished nirvana of childhood, through which we all pass, but which we must, regretfully, leave behind. It is childhood itself that seems sacrosanct and unreachable, rather than the status of being a child.

This may seem a fine distinction, but it is a crucial one. When childhood is given this aura and turned into a transient Elysium, then children are infected by the mystique. The child of the 1920s and '30s, the Edwardian child and the late Victorian child, were all inhabitants of this never-never land, rather than being the potent figures of our own times. Bare feet, romantic clothes, dreamy expressions. Indeed Carroll himself saw them thus, when he lapsed into the standard perception. The last paragraph of *Alice in Wonderland* slides into another language: 'the simple and loving heart of her childhood . . . the dream of Wonderland long ago . . . her own child-life, and the happy summer days'.

Famously, the conception of Wonderland took place on a 'golden afternoon' on the Thames near Oxford in 1862: 'the cloudless blue above, the watery mirror below, the boat drifting idly on its way, the tinkle of the drops that fell from the oars . . .' The inspiration seems to elide with that mystical concept of childhood as the lost paradise, but somewhere along the way Carroll's own idiosyncratic imaginative vision took over, vastly to our benefit, thus contributing an entire imagery and phraseology to the national culture. And a fictional child who can be interpreted to the satisfaction of generation after generation of subsequent readers.

Perhaps our radically revised view of children owes more to the demise of the designated nursery than to anything else – Freud or Spock or Bowlby or theories of *Alice*. It is one thing to see your child for an hour or so after tea (as my mother did), quite another to have them at your side twenty-four hours a day. Childhood may well be a condition apart, but unremitting contact with its peculiarities somewhat tarnishes its dreamy golden image. Most significantly, the whole relationship between adults and children has changed, reflecting the century's political inclinations. It is now much more egalitarian. Indeed, there are plenty of homes in which children would appear to have the upper hand; we jump to their tune, rather than the other way around. Their needs and requirements dictate the pattern of family life; many households, for fifteen years and more, are run to suit the children's diaries. Children are weighty consumers, the target of advertising and retailing, and are a huge financial investment: it costs around £100,000 to feed, clothe and house a child, we are told – much more if private education is involved. And the investment in terms of aspirations and expectations can never have been higher; today's children must be bright and achieving – out with docility and conformity.

A revolution in perceptions, it seems to me – the perception of children by parents, the relation of children to parents. And indeed to other adults. When we are under the same roof, my granddaughters join me in bed for a ritual early morning cup of tea and chat. For me, the notion of getting into bed with *my* grandmother would have been astonishing. Adults have lost their mystique, it would appear, their apartness, their unapproachability. And as for children, they are what they have ever been – a source of anxiety, pleasure, expense, and that genetic investment made without thought or consideration. But today's child is also viewed nervously, seen as a potential time-bomb, an unstable substance requiring the most informed and delicate handling. And thus they have acquired a power of which they must be unconsciously aware. They sense that we grown-ups walk a tightrope every day in our efforts to get things right.

So what has happened? Well, Freud happened most of all, I suppose. Certainly, Freudian theory drove childcare pundits of the Bowlby school, but the notion that childhood experience directs subsequent behaviour has reached a far wider range of parents than only those who read childcare books or know about Freud. It has somehow come to seem obvious, from the mid twentieth century onwards. Obvious, powerful and disturbing in its implications. Children are no longer seen as creatures of a different order, miniature or potential adults, but as ourselves as we once were, the alter ego that we have forgotten and cannot recover, but watch with interest.

Children are the aliens who live amongst us, deciphering our mysterious codes, learning to conform to the bizarre requirements of our society. They are Alice, the voice of reason and rationality; we adults are the cast of perverse and unpredictable characters with which she is surrounded – the White Rabbit, the Red Queen, the Mad Hatter and the rest of us. We have to view children with awe, it seems to me, as the valiant navigators who learn the language and acquire the maps, while contending with everything that is thrown at them. I'm not sure that I thought of my own children like this – too busy at the time on the rockface of child management –

but it is the vision of childhood I have since acquired, from observing and thinking. And writing for them. Writing for children seems an act of extraordinary temerity. You are offering to those without any literary tradition a product that stems from adult experience and a complex web of cultural influences. You are inviting them to share some of your concerns and interests – or at least you are if you write without patronage and from the assumption that children are not second-class citizens, but simply ourselves in this opaque and provocative other incarnation. And you have got to find a voice and a language with which to make your concerns both approachable and compelling. You can reach them through narrative; everything else that you are trying to do must be subsumed within the story, the seven-eighths of the iceberg which, you hope, will leave the child feeling that it has heard a good story but one with tantalizing and rewarding whiffs of something else, a rich and indefinable flavour.

In one corner of the big nursery at Golsoncott stood the grand piano – a huge sombre presence with a cavernous space beneath, where I once hid, when I was six, scared witless by George MacDonald's *The Princess and the Goblin*. When I look at that Victorian classic today, I can pick up an echo trace of its sinister power – not anything to be identified in the text, which now seems entirely anodyne, but some reverberation of one's own ancestral self, the child who inhabited another world, and who saw and heard things in a way that is no longer possible. Just occasionally there is a jolt of startled recognition, prompted by objects that are eerily charged with meaning. The Blüthner grand is still with the family, housed now in a light and cheerful room in north London. Watching my granddaughters play it, I feel that there should have been some counter-beam of awareness so that, crouching beneath it back then, I might have caught a rippled message from a time, place and people yet to come.

Marriage, children: the central intimacies. Matters which are entirely personal but coloured always by the customs of the day. The houses that shelter these shifting manners, all this engagement, stay the same, but not quite the same. They, too, accommodate, acknowledging the times. At Golsoncott, the dressing-room and the nursery became a spare bedroom and an artist's studio. There were no more formal wedding line-ups in the photograph albums. My grandmother's wedding dress survives, a rather tattered confection with a twenty-inch waist: her great-great-granddaughters have been allowed to try it on and very fetching they appear, if oddly out of step, their own look so much that of another time. Their childhoods are lived in a vastly different family climate. That crumpled yardage of satin and lace is an eloquent and exotic link across a hundred years. It has resonance – about how they lived then, about how we live now. Just as a house bears witness to private lives, to public events – Golsoncott, and a million other houses.

The Knife Rests, the Grape Scissors and the Bon-Bon Dish

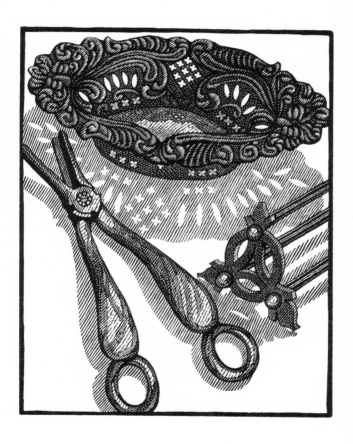

On each recovery of Golsoncott, each return to the place now safely stashed away in the mind, intact and inviolate, I review the familiar landscape of the house. A left turn out of the vestibule, past the gong stand – the cloakroom door now facing me and, behind that, the red-tiled floor, the wall of pegs slung with old raincoats, riding macs, gardening aprons, sou'westers, my aunt's hunting bowlers, the rack of walking sticks, the dog leads, everything tinged pink with Somerset earth. A right turn and into the dining-room, whose windows peer through a shroud of wisteria out across Roadwater valley towards the rolling skyline of Treborough Common and Kingsdown Clump. Here we ate and lived, during my adolescence, the arctic space of the drawing-room abandoned at the outbreak of war and reoccupied only for ceremonial occasions – Christmas Day, family christening parties, formal teas. Here in the dining-room my grandmother played Rachmaninoff and Tchaikovsky 78s that clicked and clumped from within her adventurous purchase of a radiogram. Here Rachel worked at wood engravings at the fireside. Here, each evening, I laid the table for dinner, abiding by an inexorable formula – the correct selection of implements and impedimenta from the sideboard and the silver cupboard.

For forty-five years, the sideboard was simply that, to me – an infinitely familiar object, its glass top cracked right across in one place, the right-hand cupboard devoid of its key. Sherry decanter and silver biscuit box in the left-hand cupboard, napkins and napkin rings in the top centre drawer. Now, it has acquired a further identity, alien and impersonal: the probate inventory required me to see it also as a nineteenth-century mahogany serpentine-front sideboard, with raised pierced gallery back, cross-banded border decoration, fitted central and cutlery drawers, side cupboards with ivory escutcheons, on tapering square legs and spade feet, seventy-two inches wide. Possibly. But for me it remains just the sideboard, and I know exactly where everything should be, within.

The silver cupboard was set into the wall of the pantry, a small walk-in cupboard with deep shelves and a steel door with double locks. Never locked, in my time. It had a cold metallic smell – sometimes I get a whiff of it from silverware emporia in Islington, but subtly different, because the cosseted goods on display there are far removed from the tarnished contents of the Golsoncott shelves, mostly unused and unpolished, blackened, dusty and eventually inscrutable, as we discovered when at last the place had to be dismantled.

We emptied the silver cupboard and the sideboard and spread their contents out on the dining-room table. Candlesticks, serving dishes, sugar bowls, milk jugs. Sauce boats, sugar tongs, ashtrays, salvers. Fish slices, a tea caddy, an ivory-handled crumb scoop. And other items, entirely mysterious, unseen for decades. Subliminal recognition came surging forth. Those were knife rests, that was a pair of grape scissors. And this was a bon-bon dish. 'A *what*?' said my daughter. There were the napkin rings: my grandmother's with her initials in baroque entwinement, my aunt's with her name in neat italics – *Rachel*. Her great-great-niece, aged six at the time, was helping with the glum dispersal process. You can have this, we said, because you are Rachel too. Delighted, she squirrelled the napkin ring away with her possessions. But a few minutes later she was back: 'What's it for?'

It had come to this. Time was, life could not proceed appropriately for a family such as my grandmother's without ownership of sauce ladles, knife rests and ivory-handled crumb scoops. Now her descendant did not know what a napkin ring was for. The battered and baffling array of metal in front of us seemed suddenly to be a potent symbol for eighty years of social change. It was no longer a set of once essential objects but provided the fringe furnishing of a significant narrative.

The trauma of the middle class occasioned by the death of domestic service took place during my adolescence, in the late 1940s. The wholesale departure of household servants had of course been an early effect of the outbreak of war, but the absence of staff during the war years seems to have been subsumed into the general climate of deprivation and perceived as simply one of its grimmer manifestations; in that halcyon future 'when the war is over' things would surely go back to normal. In fact, the writing had been on the wall since 1918, for anyone who cared to read it. At the turn of the century the Edwardian female domestic service workforce had numbered 2,127,000. By 1931 the census showed 1,332,000. Wages for women in domestic service and in retailing were among the lowest in all categories of employment. The 1914–18 war offered women the opportunity of work in industry – better paid and without the irritant of subservience to the gentry. The inter-war years had already seen a flight from the nation's drawing-rooms and sculleries. That said, in the early 1930s nearly one in five households still had one full-time servant living in. Most middle-class homes took it for granted that there would be someone to mind the children, do the washing-up, see to the garden.

At Golsoncott, the very architecture assumed an infrastructure of service – a medium-sized country house with one wing dedicated to kitchen, pantry and sculleries, laundry room, staff sitting-room, sewing-room, staff bathroom and bedrooms; nursery and night nursery for visiting grandchildren were in the same wing, expediently hived off from the front-ranking areas of the house. I remember lying in bed with measles in the night nursery in the summer of 1939, with the comfortable companionable sound of chatter wafting up through the floor from the kitchen. Douglas Kane, who arrived not long after in his *alter ego* of Otto Kun, describes in his memoir the full complement of staff at Golsoncott. Living in were the cook, a parlourmaid and a housemaid, both of these Swiss (and in a sense, I suppose, precursors of the au pair system of today). There was also a daily houseboy. Outdoor staff consisted of the head gardener, two under gardeners, a chauffeur and a groom. Mrs Willis came in two days a week to do the laundry.

By 1945 this entire panoply was a distant memory. At Golsoncott, there was a sense of weary accommodation. For a while, in the late forties and throughout the fifties, my grandmother attempted defiance of historic conditions. She scoured the pages of the *Lady* for 'couples' – the wife to cook, the husband to lay fires, set the table, serve, clear away and wash up, along with a good deal else. Food was the intractable problem – how to eat three times a day when to set to and provide for yourself was unthinkable. My grandmother couldn't cook anyway; my aunt had better things to do. Few of the 'couples' lasted longer than a matter of months. In the nature of things, they tended to be people who were either footloose, feckless or whose situation did not bear too close inquiry. My grandmother's letters of the period – mainly stoical, occasionally plaintive – are filled with accounts of this perpetual state of negotiation. Visitors have had to be put off because the current 'couple' have absconded, and hoped-for replacements have 'let us down'. There are dark periods of total deprivation – tins, packet soups, strange stews impatiently knocked up by Rachel, who wanted to be out in her studio, working. Rosy dawns when salvation arrived, along with proper Sunday lunch and home-made cakes for tea; disillusion as yet another pair proved dubious or inconstant.

For some odd reason, it was washing-up that mainly broke the spirit of the post-war middle class. Confronted with a sink of dirty crockery, robust women were reduced to gibbering wrecks. My grandmother would refer with shuddering sympathy to friends whose circumstances were even more straitened than her own: 'Poor dear, she is having to do all the washing-up . . .' This from a woman who thought nothing of an afternoon's heavy digging in the garden. It was not, then, that physical labour was unacceptable – simply that there was some taboo about housework. To my mind, washing-up on a normal domestic scale is a rather satisfactory job: you can see what you've achieved. For my grandmother and my aunt – both vigorous and energetic women – it was a personal affront. My aunt, younger and always more flexible in her outlook, came in time to accept the situation, though retaining a dismissive disdain for domestic chores. For my grandmother, it was the final rupture with the world in which she had grown up.

My grandmother features strongly here, and elsewhere in this book. For good reason. She is a prime source of evidence in this attempt to make a house and its time bear witness to social change over the century. Furnishings are the prompts and the props, but it is people who are the players, who drive the narrative, who give character and identity to time and place. When I summon up the late 1940s, the vision is a profoundly confusing one. There is a sense in which I am still there, a lumpen teenager, gripped by the roller-coaster emotions of that turbulent period in life. I am too tall, too tongue-tied, my hair is frizzy, my legs unshapely. I wear glasses and, down here in Somerset, where such things matter, I am no good on a horse. On the other hand, Golsoncott is the safe haven, the calm security from which I can mull over my own deficiencies, take stock of a perplexing world and undergo the slow metamorphosis into adult life.

All the while, my grandmother is an abiding presence – brisk, merry, unshakeable in her convictions. On public occasions, I take shelter behind her rock-solid confidence in the society with which she is familiar. She knows what to say when and to whom, she is never stuck for a comment or an opinion, she is deft about such stultifying embarrassments as how to locate the lavatory in an unfamiliar environment. I was devoted to her, and still am. But I was beginning to question her assumptions: about religion, about social struc-ture. We argued – good-humouredly. For my part, I was increasingly less certain that she was right about everything, though that in no way diminished my regard for her; she saw me as a normally disaffected schoolgirl who would come round to a proper outlook in due course.

In my head, my grandmother is always aged around sev-enty. Her grey hair is set in neat rolls and confined within an invisible net. She wears a tweed skirt, a blouse and cardigan in winter, linen dresses in summer. Lisle stockings, always. A large hessian apron is tied round her waist for gardening, its pockets bristling with secateurs, raffia, pruning knife. When I hugged her I could feel the carapace of her corset, never discarded, even in the hottest weather. For the evening, she changed into a long red velveteen housecoat, worn with a rope of ivory beads. Her presence seemed to animate the house. When she was out, the whole place went very still; when she was at home, her brisk step rang on the stairs and along the passages, you heard her humming and singing, you heard her laughter. She could share a joke, and had a sense of the ridiculous. But there was an implacable code of conduct, and minefields on all sides. Good manners were considered paramount – the decent consideration of each towards all. Excessive behaviour or bad language brought instant dis- approval: once, a young woman visitor, inflamed by sherry, tossed a cushion across the Golsoncott drawing-room to a friend, and was never invited to the house again. My grand- mother became tight-lipped at any sexual inference. On another occasion, when she was in her eighties, we had to leave a concert in the interval because a couple in the row in front had been kissing. Sheltered from the tabloid press, and listening only to the BBC Home Service and Third Pro- gramme, she was immune to much of the changing climate of the fifties, let alone the sixties. But occasionally the licence of the times filtered through to her; her condemnation was absolute and unrelenting. Skimpy clothing on women was a particular affront. The miniskirt made public outings an ordeal. But then, bizarrely, she rounded on the ankle-length skirts and coats of the seventies: 'Ridiculous! Why go back to all that clutter!'

That vigorous presence entirely eclipses my memory of her bedridden final years. I am glad of that. But even then, when her mind was gone and she was often in a coma, her old self would flicker to life. My husband Jack was sitting with her one day during that time, when she suddenly surfaced. She looked at him in surprise and at once became the concerned hostess:

'I'm so glad you've been able to get down to us for a few days. Are they looking after you all right?' And then a thought struck her: 'I believe my granddaughter Penelope is staying too. Have you met her? I'm sure you two would get on.'

Today, the continuous present of the late 1940s is overlaid by re-interpretations. Sometimes, it seems to have been drained of colour by the insistent imagery of old film. A raw January morning. Sunday. We are setting off for church. I can feel the itchy texture of my lisle stockings, see the metallic glint of my grandmother's dark-green chenille turban, hear the irritable cough and grunt of the Standard, which is a bad starter. In the car, the smells are of dog and damp raincoats. My grandmother remembers that she has not yet given me sixpence for the collection and passes the coin over her shoulder to me, in the back. It is cold against a chilblain on my finger. But with another pair of eyes I see that whole scene differently: the car has become very small and chunky, whisked into vintage mode, and we too are consigned to some time warp, distant stilted figures in our clothes of another era, me in my belted mac, my grandmother and aunt in their boxy tweed coats and skirts, worn only on Sundays. The past has become impersonal, redefined by film, newsprint, television documentaries, and an archive of commentary. Was I really there? Were we really thus?

But now I am the commentator, and when I see and listen to my grandmother, she has become someone conditioned by her time and place – as am I, as are we all. I have double vision: fifty years ago is both now, and then. It is all still going on, quite clear and normal, the world as I know it, but those other eyes see a frozen moment, a time of innocence: ahead lies everything that will happen to the three of us, life and death, and beneath that the shifting sands of public events. The Cold

War, the Cuban missile crisis, Vietnam. The end of Communism. The mutation of attitudes and expectations in our own country that will set in context the way we lived then.

'The most class-ridden country under the sun,' wrote George Orwell. Academic discussion of the nature of class and class distinction in Britain tends to focus on analysis: society as a hierarchy, a seamless progression from low status to high; or the triadic version with lower, middle and upper collective groups; or the dichotomy, the adversarial 'us' and 'them'. All three systems can be identified historically; all three could be identified today, depending on how you dissect society. Writing at the dawn of the twenty-first century, the climate of the early 1900s, in so far as I can apprehend it, seems alien indeed – a swirling perception derived from literature, from paintings, from photographs, from statistics. There are the facts and figures of a polarized society: before the 1914–18 war about 70 per cent of all wealth was held by the top 1 per cent of the population (by 1990 the richest 5 per cent owned 37 per cent). There are the grim conditions of the poor in London and in York as described in the pioneering surveys of Charles Booth and Seebohm Rowntree. In York, in 1901, Rowntree found that 28 per cent of the population lived at a nutritional standard below that needed to maintain mere physical health. It is the chasm between what was eaten by ordinary middle-class Edwardian households and the normal consumption of those below the poverty threshold that perhaps gives most pause for thought: the substantial, meat-heavy three-course meals of the new suburbias; the bread with jam or dripping and a pot of tea consumed three times a day by a labourer's family. Above all, it is hard now to conjure up the visible effect of this divide. In 1899 12,000 men were examined for military service. Eight thousand were rejected out of hand as failing to meet the required physical standards for infantry: height 5 feet 3 inches, chest 33 inches, weight 8 stone 3 pounds. Even in 1945, Labour members of Parliament were on average three inches shorter than Conservative members.

My grandmother was a young woman in that Edwardian society and must have experienced in old age the same double vision with which I see the 1940s. That time had the same validity for her as the mid century has for me, and she was still fingered by its customs, decades later. I doubt that she ever knew of either Booth or Rowntree and may never have appreciated that a third of the population lived at the lowest level of human tolerance, but she was a person of humanitarian instincts, whatever her social perceptions, and those raw contrasts must have been always with her. She died in 1976, aged ninety-seven, in the thick of the affluent society, amazed at the ubiquity of cars, washing-machines and foreign holidays, retaining an outdated sense of social hierarchy, but generally acknowledging a change for the better. She would have been shocked and perturbed by the street beggars of the 1990s.

My concept of the years before the Great War is derived from those stark social realities and also that imaginative view fuelled by pictures in which people are defined by dress, instantly allocated to their role and function – grandees, bourgeoisie, workers. Top hats and plumes, sober suits, overalls and aprons. The triadic version of society seems to be operating, in the mind's eye. And then there is the backdrop of literature: if these people spoke, it would be with the cadences of the Jamesian drawing-room, or Kiplingesque stylized Cockney. There is a basic accuracy to what I see, but the whole thing is overlaid by subsequent perceptions and reinterpretations. Only when you have walked in a particular world, moved from day to day, can you retrieve its essential mood.

By the time my grandmother and her family came to live at Golsoncott, the Edwardian years were dead and gone, shunted beyond the great national trauma of the war. It was the early 1920s, and the climate had changed – though in many crucial senses it remained much the same: Golsoncott was liberally serviced; life there would have been very different from that led in cottages and farmhouses round about. This was the heyday of the gong in the front hall and the panel of bells in the pantry.

When I examine my grandmother's deepest assumptions, it is her attitude towards household management that seems to be the one that removes her farthest from me. Her vision of what was normal and proper stemmed from the late nineteenth century. Mine was formed during the questioning post-war decade. At points the difference can be nicely defined by beliefs about washing-up. My grandmother considered that it should be done for her by others, and furthermore that such others would always be available, in the natural order of things; I find this viewpoint almost as inaccessible as Creationism. Admittedly, I have lived in the age of the dishwasher, but I'm not sure that technological advance negates the underlying assumption.

Social structure is a quicksand; class distinctions are unreliable and in a state of perennial reassessment. Detached discussion of such matters is endlessly absorbing; this is after all the underlying narrative of historical change. But enlightenment by way of the historians and analysts is one thing; living it out as part of the tapestry is eerily other. The patterns so clearly detectable from afar become blurred and confusing on the ground. David Cannadine has described how most Britons, when thinking about society and about themselves, are 'silently and easily shifting from one social vision to another'.

He sees the history of class in Britain as 'the history of multiple identities', a perception which seems to nail not just the complexities of retrospective analysis, but also the mercurial experience of personal involvement. We see ourselves and others differently according to whether the negotiations are daily and immediate, or by way of the impersonal climate of politics and opinion. And, above all, the social landscape is in a constant state of reconstruction.

The physical landscape of rural Somerset in the 1920s looked much the same as it does now, except that it was more populous. My aunt remembered that a morning's ride when she was a girl would bring her into contact with many neighbours, who were working the fields, travelling the lanes. By the mid century, she and I could cover miles without exchanging greetings with anyone at all. A changed regime of farming meant many fewer agricultural workers; local journeys were made by car, rather than on foot, bike or horse. But the network of social relationships that gave significance to that landscape was infinitely more ordered in the early part of the century – the structures more rigid, the contrasts stark.

The staffing set-up at Golsoncott during the twenties and thirties reflected in miniature those elaborate gradations in grander establishments, where there would have been kitchen maids and boot boys, various ranks of housemaids (up to lady's maid) and, rising onwards and upwards, cook, valets, footmen, butler and housekeeper. This is a microcosm of society as hierarchy, a system in which everyone sees themselves in relation to those above or below, and is thus perceived. Even in a group as small as that at Golsoncott there would still have been an order of seniority. And it seems obvious that for many of those in domestic service this occupational class system must have done much to obscure or displace the wider inequalities of society. If you were involved in continuous dealings with an oppressive cook or butler, then that was likely to be the focus of your resentment, rather than the more distant figures of your employers and an abstract state of affairs in which the wealthy are waited on hand and foot.

Hierarchical systems have flourished in this country. We like processions; Americans favour parades, significantly. Richard Gough's seventeenth-century church seating plan was eminently hierarchical, with the parish dignitaries in the front pews, lesser ranks behind, cottagers at the back. And within the parameters of the triadic structure – upper, middle and lower classes – are internal hierarchies: the rankings of the peerage, the ornate classifications within the professional classes that were a strong feature of the early part of the twentieth century, the subtle gradations of status within the old working class. My husband Jack grew up on a Newcastle-upon-Tyne council estate in the 1930s and could describe graphically the system of mutual assessment within his street; the engine-driver, commanding universal respect on account of his occupation; the family known to be always behind with the rent; the brawny matriarch, who policed the activities of roaming children and provided up-to-date information on who had acquired what and whose husband was out of work. Aspirations and comparisons are always centred upon those nearest to us; the more prosperous neighbour is an immediate object of interest and envy, whereas the unimaginable wealth of the stately home owner is so far removed as to be irrelevant for practical purposes. Hierarchical systems and customs have traditionally shored up class distinction.

At the start of the new century, they are eroded by some degree of redistribution of wealth and, essentially, by consumer goods. Except for those at the top or bottom of the scale, most Britons eat much the same food, wear similar clothes, drive the same makes of car, the decay or otherwise of which is probably now the most potent signal of income (or inclination). Where and how a person lives tells you much, but no longer everything. And a street crowd today is far removed from that of the 1900s or even a quarter of a century later, when details of dress and appearance could nail pretty well everyone.

None of which means that we have achieved the classless society so blithely invoked by politicians. Indeed, the very fact that prime ministers of both political parties have gone in for aspirational talk of the classless society over recent years suggests that they are well aware that it is not yet with us.

Half a century ago, at Golsoncott, the bon-bon dish, the salver, the ivory-handled crumb scoop and the rest of all that symbolic metalware went into retirement; an obscure local non-event reflected a changing national climate. The place adjusted, as buildings do. It became very cold, in a world growing accustomed to central heating. The house contracted to an occupied heartland amid infrequently visited territories where things went their own way. By the 1980s the wisteria had sent leafy tendrils into the drawing-room and there was a magnificent wasps' nest in the attic sewing-room. The old nursery had long since become my aunt's studio. The enforced simplification rather suited her; she had never set much store by domestic niceties, preferred anyway to sleep under a tarpaulin on an open-sided balcony, and was relieved to be excused the tyranny of set mealtimes. Outside, only its bone structure and a number of tenacious growths were a reminder of what the garden had once been. The rose beds in the terrace were turfed over, the irises in the canal garden had dwindled away, bulrushes choked the canal itself. But the choisya bushes flourished, the *Fuchsia magellanica* showered down around the pasture that had been the tennis court, the rare hydrangea species in the front of the house grew sturdier by the year, and *Erigeron karvinskianus* was exuberant.

In 1995 there was still a tin of Silvo at the back of the silver cupboard, its contents long since dried up, unused for many a year. Eloquent of household change, but with further resonances in time and space. Silvo was, and is, made by Reckitt and Colman, the Hull-based industrial concern. Its use at Golsoncott was not just expedient but also a matter of loyalty. My grandfather, Norman Reckitt, was a grandson of the founder of the firm, Isaac Reckitt, an archetypal Victorian industrial entrepreneur. Trade, in other words: in the subtle hierarchy of the Victorian and Edwardian upper and middle classes the family would have been put firmly in its place. My grandfather was an architect and had no active involvement in the firm, but his son Basil was a director and ultimately the chairman. My information on the fortunes of the firm is drawn from his history, published in 1951. That defunct tin of Silvo evokes another world – that of timely industrial exploitation of the population's abiding demand for household cleaning products.

There is something neatly appropriate about Reckitt & Sons' products in any discussion of social change, wedded as they are to the nation's domestic circumstances. Starch, grate cleaner, metal polishes: the goods reflect an age and a lifestyle. An advertisement of 1939 (illustrated in Basil Reckitt's book) catches perfectly both the time and the tone. A buxom, aproned sixty-something passes an appreciative hand across what looks like a fine damask tablecloth: 'This is a lovely bit of work, Mum! It's just as well you've Mrs Rawlins by you when you've things in the wash like this. Heirlooms, I call them. Not that I can do anything more than what I've already told you, Mum. Pop it into my Reckitt's Blue so that it comes out dazzling. And when I come to the ironing, I've my Robin Starch . . .' the caption runs on for quite a while; Reckitt's seem to have been in the forefront of early twentieth-century product advertising (indeed, a film was made featuring Mrs Rawlins, played by the comedy actress May Brough) but had not arrived at the snappy soundbite.

Robin Starch was the descendant of the firm's original product, first produced back in the 1840s. On the wall of my London study today hang small reproduction portraits of my great-great-grandparents, Isaac and Ann Reckitt. Born in the 1790s, they had a foot in the eighteenth century, took advantage of the industrial boom of the high Victorian period, and laid the foundations of a twentieth-century industry. They were Quakers; Ann Reckitt, in her portrait, wears the white mob cap favoured by Quaker women. Isaac started life in Lincolnshire and operated initially as a flour miller; poor harvests and tumbling grain prices forced diversification and, in 1840, the family moved to Hull, where the starch manufactory was set up. The early years were hard going and the business survived only because Isaac was equipped with that vital asset of the private entrepreneur – sons. George, Francis and James, three of the boys, did gruelling stints as travelling salesmen while still in their teens, pressing samples of Soluble Starch into the hands of the innumerable small grocers upon whose favour the business would depend. The fourth son, Frederick, worked on site. Gradually, the business went into profit. New lines were added; by 1854 the list of products, though still dominated by the various starches, included Reckitt's Power Blue and Reckitt's Azure Ball Blue, along with several lines in Black Lead. After the 1914–18 war, Reckitt and

Sons' main products were still starch and blue, along with grate and metal polishes. Isaac's astute enterprise had paved the way for the firm's invasion of the nation's kitchens and sculleries by way of Robin Starch, Reckitt's Blue, Brasso, Silvo, Zebra polish and, eventually, Dettol.

Starch. The very word conjures up for me a tactile pleasure unknown to today's children. Bone-white powder that you mixed with a little water to make a smooth and glistening paste with a squeaky texture, which stiffened to a fascinating chalky solidity. I remember being allowed to mess about with it on washing days. I remember too the crackle of a pristine starched sheet, and the crisp cotton frocks of my childhood. Laundry was taken seriously, back then.

Reckitt & Sons took it extremely seriously, to good effect. Washday products were the core of the business; an early excursion into biscuits generated little profit and thereafter cleaning products were the mainstay, with the expedient acquisition of competitors a prime concern as the business prospered. In the decade before the 1914–18 war, Reckitt & Sons gobbled up the Bluebell and Shinio companies – rivals in the brass-polish trade – along with a handful of other competitors, thus sweeping in some useful household-name products such as Cherry Blossom and Mansion. Major employers on Humberside, and now expanding overseas, they were a significant force in early twentieth-century industry; Isaac Reckitt's bold little business half a century earlier seems suddenly very far away. The stern-faced men in Board photographs are still predominantly Reckitts – there was always a convenient supply of sons – but the firm became more impersonal as it joined the mainstream of national industrial history.

Isaac and his sons seem the very essence of mid nineteenth-century commercial determination. Their energy – the boys trekking the north-east by rail (third class) and coach, dossing down in cheap boarding-houses. Their enterprise – experimenting with new products. Not always successfully, as when a dietetic arrowroot made from farina and intended to act as a substitute for real arrowroot (used as an invalid drink) was confidently offered to a potential middleman but failed to cool into a jelly, as required, exposing George to considerable embarrassment. They were quick to spot the importance of brand promotion: 'Hast thou seen to the large placard being printed yet in London and hast thou prepared the wording for it?' writes Francis to George. 'How would this do: "Try the newly discovered Starch called Reckitt's Imperial Wheaten Starch, which for its great strength, for the brilliance of its colour, the splendid glaze which it imparts to the linen and the ease with which it is used surpasses any other"?' And there is the streak of creativity that could prompt moves such as the dispatch of a quantity of starch to the Russian Emperor Nicholas I in 1850. The idea behind this was to interest the Chief Laundress in the Imperial Household, with an eye to a testimonial, and to this end Isaac entered into personal negotiations with the captain of the ship carrying the cargo to St Petersburg, who allegedly had a contact in the palace. Amazingly, the scheme worked. After pursuing inquiries with the Russian Consulate in London, 'Messrs Rickett' received a gracious acknowledgement a year later, enabling a subsequent advertising campaign to list among Reckitt's distinctions 'The supply of the Imperial Laundry of the EMPEROR OF ALL THE RUSSIAS' and, what's more, 'The supply of the Imperial Laundry of His Majesty the Emperor LOUIS NAPOLEON III'. A further and similar approach had been made; emperors were now seen as fair game. But why not our own dear Queen?

There was a late flare of this creative thinking in 1927 (by which time Isaac's grandsons were directors of the company). A general decline in demand for the main Reckitt products was necessitating diversification – eventually into pharmaceuticals, and the ubiquitous disinfectant, Dettol. But the significantly reduced call for Brasso was giving particular pause for thought. The reason for this fall was that modern houses had fewer fittings which required polishing – door-handles and so forth. In an attempt to distract attention from this basic problem, the company set about a campaign to popularize the use of ornamental brassware, including the sale of specially com-missioned goods by their own reps through the traditional channel of the small local grocery store. A neat idea, if some-thing of a last-ditch stand.

Isaac Reckitt was in most respects a stereotypical nine-teenth-century entrepreneur. Conditions in his Hull works would have been similar to those up and down the country: long hours and minimal wages. Indeed, the twelve-hour day worked by the female employees during the latter half of the century would seem to be in contravention of the 1847 Ten Hour Act. But he was also a Quaker. The benevolent paternal-ism of the Quaker industrialist was a feature of the firm from an early stage. There were education classes for girls during working hours (maybe that accounts for the twelve-hour day) and, in the 1900s, a Social Hall had been provided, along with a Girls' Rest Room, and a works' doctor and dentist.

These provisions arrived during the reign of Isaac's youngest son James. But his most enlightened contribution was the building of the Garden Village – 600 houses to be reserved mainly for employees of Reckitt's. Here he was operating very much according to the lights of the other leading Quaker industries – Rowntree's, Fry's and especially Cadbury's, whose Bournville Village Trust on the (then) outskirts of Birmingham must surely have been the inspiration – along with the whole garden-city movement of the time.

This discursion into industrial history seems a far cry from the domestic intimacies of a house in the most rural reaches of the West Country. Concealed resonances, once again. The contents of the Golsoncott silver cupboard are peculiarly eloquent in conjuring up a way of life and its accompanying ideologies. Many of these are completely mysterious to me – I wasn't around when all this was going on. But some were the backdrop to my own beginnings. Then I was there myself, in the thick of these practices, too young to do much but accept and record. And what was recorded is now blurred by subsequent understanding.

Our early assumptions and beliefs are archaeological debris and their retrieval is almost as difficult, and quite as haphazard, as the recovery of the vision of childhood. What did I think before I learned how to think? How did I receive ideas before I discovered scepticism? Within any of us there is a host of strangers – the people we no longer are but with whom we feel an eerie affinity. Sometimes they wave a hand in greeting; we recognize them with surprise, unease, distaste or kindly patronage.

The society of the late forties and early fifties in which I was young seems cut and dried in a way that today's is not, and that perhaps none could ever be again. It seems thus both through the prism of subsequent analysis and comment, and by way of my own uneven recollection. Here and there, things come into sharp focus; I know what I saw and felt and I know that it is not what I see and feel today. That world was one in which people were much clearer about who they were, and who others were. The definitions of occupation, speech and dress were a straitjacket on attitudes and assumptions. For a novelist, the most valuable rule when observing other people is to tell yourself that nothing is ever what it seems. Back then, things were all too often just what they seemed. At nineteen or twenty, I, too, wore a uniform that placed me (within what was, admittedly, a pretty broad constituency): female, respectable, reasonably well-heeled. Skirt with blouse, sweater or cardigan; raincoat on top, or tweed coat in winter; suit or frock for best. It was a uniform that made no concessions to youth, being a mirror image of that worn by a woman of forty, fifty or sixty. I certainly didn't look like the student that I was. At Oxford, some of us occasionally wore prototype jeans (not denim, which was not yet much around, but limp blue affairs) and felt rather dashing, but we wouldn't have dreamed of wearing them to a lecture or tutorial. The men were uniformed in brown duffel coats and grey flannels; girls wore skirts and sweaters by day, and got done up in strapless frocks for parties. I remember one contemporary who always put on hat and gloves to go to the Bodleian; however, we free spirits thought that a touch formal. But I had been plagued by gloves, as an adolescent. They had to be worn or carried on all but the most informal outings; without them, it seemed, my station in life would not be apparent. Puzzled but biddable, I spent several years losing slimy nylon objects until eventually liberated by student life and common sense.

Social and occupational uniforms are still around, but those wearing them may no longer conform to expectations. My father worked in the City. I remember going to meet him there one evening, when I was about sixteen. Emerging from Bank tube station, I found myself amid a throng of father-clones – droves of men wearing his suit, his bowler hat, carrying his furled umbrella, indistinguishable. I arrived at our rendezvous in a fit of giggles, and was soundly ticked off. My father was a man with a robust sense of humour, but the insignia of office were no laughing matter, in 1949. Looking back, it seems as though there was some unease and insecurity beneath the surface, forcing a need for identifying paraphernalia, in all classes. In a society that is given to classification, you need to establish your credentials, lest you become displaced. My grandmother would occasionally say of some acquaintance, in perplexity: 'I find her rather hard to place.' Today, a whole swathe of the population is unplaceable, and would prefer to remain so.

Post-war social reform focused upon opportunity – educational above all. How far this has come about is a matter of statistics, but is also essentially a question of climate. Social mobility can be quantified, to a degree: you establish a definition of class structure, investigate who springs from where, and thus discover how many people move up and down from the class into which they were born. By the late 1970s, 44 per cent of the post-war generation could be shown to have been socially mobile; an expanding middle class was absorbing those from 'below', and occasionally from 'above'. Behind the bald figures lies the social metamorphosis – the emergence of a revised set of assumptions and expectations. And the expression of such change is that shifting vision experienced by any of us who have lived through these times.

My father's bowler hat would be an anachronism today. And I could not pick out an individual from a tube-station crowd – at Bank or anywhere else – and arrive with absolute certainty at their occupation or background. Distinctions in dress seem to be cultural now, rather than social; I can analyse the tourists in a London street by their clothes, as often as not – the cut of a continental jacket or raincoat, the transatlantic style. Home-grown uniforms nowadays are largely those imposed upon us by the rag trade and chain stores.

I cannot recover the certainties of the mid century and in any case they were not certainties for me, because when you are young your natural inclination is to question the status quo – bowler hats inspire laughter rather than recognition. But I can recover the format of that time – its structures and its preconceptions. I would not want to go back there. It was a world constrained by assumptions. Assumptions about others; assumptions about oneself. The shape of a spoken word, the rise and fall of a sentence – pigeon-holes were waiting, the listener made an instant and automatic allocation. I was conditioned into tramline expectations of others and also into corresponding assumptions about myself; piece by piece, this conditioning was eroded by a changing climate and by the enlightenment of experience until, fifty years on, it is almost irretrievable.

The glass-fronted bookcase in the Golsoncott study housed a set of bound volumes of *Punch*, reaching back to the 1880s. The ultimate in languid contentment was a summer afternoon spent lounging on the veranda swing seat with a volume from around 1926 that I had not revisited lately, so that it had become somewhat unfamiliar. The text was so arcane as to defeat me entirely; the cartoons I devoured, but found them more and more baffling the further back in time I went. It was the in-built social comment that was impenetrable to my fourteen- or fifteen-year-old *alter ego*, I now realize. Not to mention the turn-of-the-century style, whereby a sequence of exchanges pile ponderously to a climax. By the twenties and thirties the jokes were somewhat more slimline, but still gave pause for thought – Mistress: 'Can you let us have dinner rather earlier?'; New Cook: 'Lor, yes. I'll just turn the gas a bit higher!' Why was that funny?

Such cartoons remain distinctly unfunny today, considered in the detachment of the British Library's Reading Room. A far cry from the Golsoncott veranda, but the red-gold tomes are eerily familiar. And, now, the culture there presented is a revelation rather than a perplexity. The sociology of *Punch* requires wisdoms of interpretation. That said, I see now also that one of its fascinations, back then, was precisely my confused awareness that something odd was going on here. A dim perception of processes of change – that 1890 was a long way from 1920 and even further from 1940. A visitation of other times and places where things were seen and done differently.

The mistress-and-cook cartoon is typical of a vein of servant jokes that runs right through the twenties and thirties, in which the servant is usually portrayed as amusingly naïve, or, as a variation, obtuse or impertinent. The quaint turn of phrase of the working class is a favourite theme – Visitor: 'How is Mrs Brown today?'; Maid: 'Well, 'm, she ebbs and flows.' Indeed, most jokes hinging on an exchange between middle- and working-class figures focus on mutual incomprehension, with the working-class character serving normally as the butt. Though there is an interesting variant in the country yokel figure, who may also discountenance his middle-class interlocutor, as with the motorist of 1925 seeking directions from an unforthcoming local – the motorist snaps in exasperation, 'Well, you don't seem to know much.' To which the riposte is: 'Maybe not, but I ain't lost.'

Class is an obsession. But there is an obsessive quality to much of the humour. The same themes crop up again and again. Tramps – usually possessed of earthy or innocent wit. (Can tramps have been such a feature of the early twentieth-century landscape?) Burglars – invariably masked and wearing striped sweaters. Surprisingly, they are still around in the 1950 volumes, along with that other hardy perennial, the Silly Little Woman. Gender is as abiding a topic as class; women are uninformed, literal-minded, extravagant and foolish. Men are fanatical about sport (golf, usually), barricade themselves behind the newspaper at breakfast and are no match for flighty or dismissive girls – the disastrous proposal is a favoured subject.

Punch has ever been the telling expression of middle England. Those between-the-wars numbers are peculiarly rewarding – and perplexing – in their evocation of a vanished world and extinguished preoccupations. Fox-hunting. There is a hunting joke in every issue, it seems, often combining that theme with some form of social comment – as in the post-war sportsman of the early twenties, a parvenu who drops his 'h's and makes social gaffes. Big-game hunting, too, is a rich topic; environmental concern is so far distant as to be apparently inconceivable. Similarly cars and drivers (especially women drivers) – though here there is a whisper of future unease, with the car (frequently broken down) featuring as the invader of idyllic landscapes.

All this seems startlingly archaic now. By the 1950s I was on the scene, but the *Punch* climate of that decade is today as alien as those of the earlier ones. By the mid century there are jokes about washing-machines (clueless husbands load them with dirty crockery) and television, but the tone and style are of an unreachable world. They are as disconcerting as the clipped and urgent tones of the radio announcers and newsreel commentators of the day; did people really speak thus, and did we truly hear them without surprise? That teenager on the Golsoncott veranda is indeed someone else.

★

This book has tried to use the furnishings of a house as a mnemonic system. I have always been excited and intrigued by the silent eloquence of the physical world – past events locked into the landscape or lurking in city streets. Every house tells a story. Golsoncott's story spans much of the century; it is personal but also public. Historical change determined how life was lived there; objects can be made to bear witness. In the process, a maverick form of social comment seems to emerge – the house becomes a secret mirror of the times, arbitrary and selective, reflecting shafts of light from unexpected directions. Decoding, interpreting, I have been made to consider the view from the house when I was sixteen, and compare it with the world of today.

Fifty years on, our society is apparently less structured, more open, more tolerant; it provides opportunities. Or is it? Does it? And was that mid century climate quite as unrelenting as it now seems? Looking around – looking back – I begin to wonder. There's not so much to be complaisant about today. This country remains polarized; insolent wealth is still there, so is abysmal poverty. The standard class distinctions are holding up – economic, social, political. We still define ourselves, and others, as we shift from one category to another. But the categories have themselves been redefined, over the years. The consensual politics of the twentieth century's end are a far cry from the appositions of earlier decades. We are all sited on the middle ground now, or at least most of us are. There is still a social spectrum, but the location of a person or a group is more difficult: both can have chameleon quality, or resist assignment. Old wealth is still evident, but the inflated incomes that invite envy or distaste are those of the corporate buccaneers or city traders and the stars of sport and entertainment – the new economic plutocracy.

The brave foundation of the post-war welfare state has been steadily undermined. Education above all provokes a degree of despair – here we are with, still, a flourishing private sector patronized for good reason by many parents who might prefer to do otherwise; the alternative is frequently alarming. Until the state system is so good that middle-class parents cease to opt out of it, it is hard to see how private education will ever waste away. And education is at the heart of change: the essential right.

Considered thus, it can seem as though there have been some superficial adjustments to the social landscape – nothing more. Scratch the surface and the basic structure is still much the same. And yet . . . When I take the central event of my own life, significantly placed in the middle of the century, I realize that right there is a potent indicator of a much more seismic disturbance. Marriage. Quite simply, the marriage of two people who could never have met in a previous age. In 1957 I married Jack Lively; a girl from the southern gentry, a young man from the northern working class. We met in Oxford, in the clear blue air of higher education, both of us freed from the assumptions and expectations of our backgrounds. At the time, it all seemed a purely private and personal matter; only subsequently can I see what we owed to a stealthy revolution, and be grateful.

Acknowledgements

I am grateful to Ann and Anthony Thwaite for reading the manuscript and for making valuable comments and suggestions, and to my family for their interest and support.

This book is not a work of scholarship; I feel that to cite all of its many sources would be inappropriate. The British Library has been my mainstay. An abbreviated bibliography follows.

Bibliography

Britnieva, Mary, *One Woman's Story* (Arthur Baker, London, 1934)

——, *A Stranger in Your Midst* (Arthur Baker, London, 1936)

Cannadine, David, *Class in Britain* (Yale University Press, London, 1998)

Carr, Raymond, *English Fox Hunting: A History* (Weidenfeld & Nicolson, London, 1976)

Coats, Alice M., *The Quest for Plants: A History of the Horticultural Explorers* (Studio Vista, London, 1969)

Gough, Richard, *The History of Myddle*, ed. David Hey (Penguin, Harmondsworth, 1981)

Inglis, Ruth, *The Children's War: Evacuation 1939–45* (Collins, London, 1989)

Mabey, Richard, *Flora Britannica* (Sinclair-Stevenson, London, 1996)

Musgrave, Toby, Gardner, Chris, and Musgrave, Will, *The Plant Hunters: Two Hundred Years of Adventure and Discovery Around the World* (Ward Lock, London, 1998)

Reckitt, Basil N., *The History of Reckitt & Sons Limited* (A. Brown & Sons, London, 1951)

Stevenson, John, *British Society 1914–45* (Allen Lane, Harmondsworth, 1984)

Yates, Frances A., *The Art of Memory* (Routledge and Kegan Paul, London, 1966)